PENGUIN PASSNOTES

Julius Caesar

Neil Taylor, M.A. (Cantab.), M.A. (Birmingham),
has considerable experience of teaching from
O-level to degree level and is at present Senior
Lecturer in English at the Roehampton Institute.
Most of his publications have been on Shakespeare
and other Elizabethan dramatists.

PENGUIN PASSNOTES

WILLIAM SHAKESPEARE
Julius Caesar

NEIL TAYLOR
ADVISORY EDITOR: STEPHEN COOTE, M.A., PH.D.

PENGUIN BOOKS

Penguin Books Ltd, Harmondsworth, Middlesex, England
Viking Penguin Inc., 40 West 23rd Street, New York, New York 10010, U.S.A.
Penguin Books Australia Ltd, Ringwood, Victoria, Australia
Penguin Books Canada Ltd, 2801 John Street, Markham, Ontario, Canada L3R 1B4
Penguin Books (N.Z.) Ltd, 182–190 Wairau Road, Auckland 10, New Zealand

First published 1985

Made and printed in Great Britain by
Richard Clay (The Chaucer Press) Ltd, Bungay, Suffolk
Filmset in Monophoto Ehrhardt by
Northumberland Press Ltd, Gateshead

*The publishers are grateful to the following Examination Boards for
permission to reproduce questions from examination papers used in
individual titles in the Passnotes series:*

*Associated Examining Board, University of Cambridge Local Examinations
Syndicate, Joint Matriculation Board, University of London School
Examinations Department, Oxford and Cambridge Schools Examination
Board, University of Oxford Delegacy of Local Examinations.*

*The Examination Boards accept no responsibility whatsoever for the
accuracy or method of working in any suggested answers given as models.*

Contents

To the Student

This book is designed to help you with your O-level or C.S.E. English Literature examinations. It contains an introduction to the play, analysis of scenes and characters, and a commentary on some of the issues raised by the play. Line references are to the New Penguin Shakespeare, edited by Norman Sanders.

When you use this book remember that it is no more than an aid to your study. It will help you find passages quickly and perhaps give you some ideas for essays. But remember: *This book is not a substitute for reading the play and it is your response and your knowledge that matter.* These are the things the examiners are looking for, and they are also the things that will give you the most pleasure. Show your knowledge and appreciation to the examiner, and show them clearly.

Introduction: Background to Julius Caesar

The central event in Shakespeare's play is the assassination of Julius Caesar. It occurs at the moment in Caesar's career when he is at his most powerful and successful. He has been awarded a ten-year Dictatorship of Rome, and is also celebrating his recent victory in Spain over the sons of his old enemy, Pompey the Great.

But Caesar is being encouraged by close supporters, such as Mark Antony, to acquire even more power by having himself crowned king. Shakespeare does not tell us what Caesar thinks of this idea. But Caesar is probably only waiting for the most advantageous moment to take this step, which will change Rome from a Republic into a Monarchy.

Meanwhile, disaffected former supporters of Pompey, led by Cassius and Brutus, are planning a coup. They believe that the Republic can be saved only if they strike before Caesar assumes absolute power. Who will get there first? The 'Monarchists' or the 'Republicans'? The first half of the play is marked by mounting suspense.

Cassius and Brutus decide to act when Caesar is about to address the Senate. Being Senators themselves they are standing near him as he takes his place in the Senate House. He is at their mercy. Suddenly they kill him, in cold blood and in the full gaze of the public. It has the sickening horror of any political killing, but it is more dramatic than most, for Caesar is killed by those he knows to be his colleagues, even by those he counts as his close friends. And they don't run away. They stand their ground and seek the approval of those who have witnessed the deed.

In the second half of the play, we observe the consequences of the assassination, the struggle for power between the conspirators and those who oppose them out of loyalty to the dead Caesar – Antony, Lepidus and Caesar's heir, Octavius. We see the conspirators driven out of the city, and we see the deaths of Brutus and Cassius at Philippi. The play ends with Antony and Octavius triumphant. If we know anything of Roman history we know that Octavius will go on to become Emperor of Rome, assuming just the kind of absolute power that Brutus had committed murder to prevent Julius Caesar acquiring.

Despite its title, the play is not built around one character. Caesar is dead in the third Act. Nor is he presented as anything of a hero – he suffers from deafness and epilepsy, and he is vain, self-important and inconsistent.

Brutus is the most interesting character. He is sensitive, intelligent and high-principled. Nevertheless he decides to commit murder in the interests of a political ideal. Once Caesar is dead, we see Brutus making crucial, even fatal, decisions. We see him suddenly out-manouevred by his enemies, involved in a complex and emotional quarrel with Cassius, and then leading his troops into a war which he proceeds to lose. We see him visited in the middle of the night by the ghost of Caesar. We see him in the act of suicide.

On the other hand, a third character makes something of a bid to be considered the major actor of, at least, the second half of the play. Until the assassination, Mark Antony says almost nothing and hardly appears on the stage. But after the assassination he almost immediately takes control of events. He commits himself to revenge, and acts with immense dynamism and cunning.

Julius Caesar is thus concerned with a cluster of characters, each of whom embodies remarkable and often conflicting personal traits, and each of whom is involved in important and dramatic events. But the action of the play centres not on character so much as on a tragic process. That process includes the fulfilment and the demolition of individuals' hopes and ambitions. But it does not only affect individuals. The whole of Rome is thrown into confusion, civil war breaks out, and some of the city's most talented sons are killed. It is a *tragic* process because, as well as being destructive and painful, there is a logic to the sequence of events. We may be appalled at the waste of life and talent, but we can see why, given the natures of those involved – Caesar,

Cassius, Brutus, Antony, the crowd, and so on – and given the political situation in which they are enmeshed at the start of the play, Rome should have to undergo this calamitous period in its history.

Synopsis

It is the Feast of Lupercus, the god of shepherds. Julius Caesar has chosen this day to celebrate his recent victory over the sons of his old enemy, the late Pompey the Great, and will be passing in triumph through the streets of Rome. The play opens with a scene in which a crowd of workers has gathered in the street to see the procession. But their representatives in the government of Rome, the Tribunes of the People, reveal themselves to have been supporters of Pompey rather than Caesar. These Tribunes, Marullus and Flavius, consequently drive the crowd off the streets and set about removing all the street decorations so that Caesar's procession will seem a failure. (They are later arrested and put to death for this action.)

We move to another street (I, ii). Part of the annual celebrations of the Lupercalia was the tradition that young men should run naked through the streets clearing a path by playfully striking those in the crowd who blocked the way. Mark Antony, Caesar's favourite, has been chosen as one of the young men and Caesar, who now enters the stage at the head of the triumphal procession, halts and calls him up to speak to him. Caesar asks Antony to make sure that he touches Calphurnia as he runs the 'holy chase', for Caesar superstitiously believes his wife's barrenness may be cured in this way. Before the procession can continue a Soothsayer calls on Caesar from the crowd and warns him to beware the Ides (the 15th) of March. Caesar seems uninterested, and the procession moves off the stage leaving behind just two of its members. These are Brutus and Cassius, who are brothers-in-law, Senators, and former supporters of Pompey. We soon discover that they also share a fear that Caesar has gained too much power.

Cassius accuses Brutus of being withdrawn and unfriendly. Brutus apologizes and explains that he has been preoccupied by his own problems, but Cassius believes he can detect in Brutus' moodiness and the fact that he has abandoned Caesar's procession a deep distaste for Caesar's growing power and personal aggrandisement. When they hear shouts off-stage Brutus instinctively exclaims 'What means this shouting? I do fear the people/Choose Caesar for their king' (ll. 79–80) and thereby gives the game away. Brutus does indeed fear that Caesar may soon be given the absolute power that would go with the transformation of Rome from a Republic into a Monarchy.

Cassius' opposition to Caesar seems to be more personal than that of Brutus. It is primarily a matter of envy and contempt for the man himself. Brutus has no hatred for Caesar. Indeed, he is his friend. But Brutus opposes him on the principle that Caesar has come to represent a threat to the continued existence of the Republic. Cassius hopes to persuade Brutus to join a conspiracy to assassinate Caesar but, as yet, Brutus is hesitant, unwilling to face the bloody consequences of the political principle he supports.

Caesar's procession passes by and it is evident from the looks on the faces of Caesar, Calphurnia and Cicero that something has upset them. Brutus pulls at the sleeve of one of the Senators in the procession and encourages him to stay behind and explain what has been happening to Caesar. This Senator is Casca, who shares Cassius' contempt for Caesar.

Casca describes how Antony offered Caesar the crown three times and each time the crowd cheered as Caesar rejected it. But Casca believes that Caesar was only play-acting to please the crowd and in truth wanted to accept. He further describes how Caesar then fell down in an epileptic fit. Before going, Casca adds that Flavius and Marullus have been executed for their attempts to spoil Caesar's triumph. Brutus leaves Cassius alone, and Cassius plots to win his support for the conspiracy by sending him anonymous letters in different hands encouraging his opposition to Caesar.

In the next scene (I, iii) it is the night before the Ides of March. Shakespeare ignores the fact that the Feast of Lupercus (the day of

Caesar's triumphal procession) was on February 13, i.e. a whole month ago. He manages to give the impression that this scene takes place only a few hours after I, ii.

The night is a wild one, a thunderstorm is raging and we learn from Casca of unnatural portents which frighten him and others whom he has met in the streets. Cicero hurries off to the safety of his home but Cassius, who enters next, is fearless of the storm and portents. He tells Casca that if Caesar really intends to accept the crown next day in the Capitol he is prepared to kill him. Casca makes it clear that he is prepared to join such an enterprise. Another conspirator, Cinna, hurries in looking for Cassius, who immediately despatches him to plant counterfeit letters enticing Brutus to join them. Cassius and Casca are confident that the conspiracy will prosper. Brutus has a large popular following, and they are convinced that he will join them.

It is now (II, i) just after midnight and Brutus is unable to sleep. He is thinking through the reasons why he fears Caesar is going to accept the crown and thereby become a threat to the liberty of all Roman citizens. His conclusion is that whatever his virtues Caesar must be stopped, and that this means he must be killed.

Lucius, Brutus' young servant, brings him a letter which has just been thrown in the window. It exhorts Brutus to 'Speak, strike, redress!' He has already received a number of anonymous letters and fails to realize that Cassius is behind them all. Therefore he takes this letter to be evidence that he is far from alone in believing that Caesar must die.

There is a knock at the door and the other conspirators enter – Cassius, Casca, Decius, Cinna, Metellus and Trebonius. Brutus shakes their hands and speaks to them of the high moral principles (the overthrow of tyranny, the purification of political life in Rome) underlying his conception of the conspiracy. Brutus goes on to persuade them not to invite Cicero to join them and also not to kill Mark Antony with Caesar. At three a.m., with dawn breaking, Brutus' visitors leave him, agreeing to meet at Caesar's house at eight a.m. in order to escort him, like friends, to the Capitol. Brutus' wife, Portia, then comes down to ask him why he has not been in bed and why he has acted so strangely over the last few days. She asks him to trust her with his secrets, but before he can say anything another conspirator, Ligarius, arrives at the door. He is ill, but when he hears that Brutus has agreed to join the plot to assassinate Caesar he eagerly urges Brutus to lead him to Caesar's house. Thunder can be heard as they leave.

Caesar, too, has been unable to sleep (II, ii). Quite apart from the storm, Caesar has been kept awake by Calphurnia, whose dreams have frightened her into believing that her husband is in mortal danger. Caesar has his priests examine the entrails of a freshly killed animal: they bring alarming news that the beast proves to be totally lacking in one organ, the heart. Calphurnia has persuaded Caesar not to go to the Senate House, but when the conspirator Decius arrives he easily changes Caesar's mind. By eight a.m. a group of Senators has gathered to accompany Caesar to the Capitol. They include the loyal Antony as well as men like Brutus whom we know intend to murder Caesar within a few hours.

In a brief scene (II, iii), Artemidorus intends to stand in the street and give Caesar a letter warning him of the conspiracy against his life and naming those who make up the plot.

It is now nine a.m. (II, iv). Because she seems to know what Brutus intends to do, Portia is full of anxiety. She is eager for news of the success or failure of the conspiracy, but afraid to let her servant boy become aware of what is afoot. She comes across a Soothsayer intent on warning Caesar that he is in danger. Nearly fainting with worry she tells the boy to run to the Senate House and quickly report back on anything he sees happening there.

With a flourish of trumpets Caesar leads the crowd of Senators into the Senate House (III, i). As he goes in he acknowledges the Soothsayer and Artemidorus, but ignores the Soothsayer's warning and refuses to read Artemidorus' letter. While Trebonius deliberately draws Antony away from Caesar, Metellus Cimber presents Caesar with a petition that his brother's banishment be repealed. Caesar refuses to hear Metellus' argument, protesting that once he has decided something he is 'constant as the northern star' (l. 60) and cannot be persuaded to change his mind. Brutus adds his voice to that of Metellus Cimber, then Cassius adds his too. When Caesar still proves adamant Cinna and Decius add their voices to the others, prompting Caesar to grow increasingly angry. This is the crisis of the play. In the growing crescendo of voices Casca pushes forward and, crying 'Speak hands for me!' (III, i, 76), stabs Caesar. All the other conspirators follow suit. As he collapses, Caesar is horrified to see that his friend Brutus should be among his assassins. He cries out in Latin, '*Et tu, Brute?*' But Brutus goes on to deliver the death blow and Caesar falls to the ground.

With Caesar dead at their feet the conspirators are jubilant. They cry out that they have secured liberty for Rome and, at Brutus' prompting, smear their hands and forearms in Caesar's blood. Antony had fled at the moment of the brutal killing, but he now sends a request to Brutus for an interview and explanation of the reasons why Caesar was put to death. Despite Cassius' doubts, Brutus agrees to Antony's request.

Antony makes clear his loyalty to the dead Caesar, but when Brutus and Cassius assure him that he will have a place in the new government of Rome he shakes the hand of each conspirator in turn and promises them his friendship. He merely asks permission to speak at Caesar's funeral, and, again ignoring Cassius' advice, Brutus agrees to the request.

Left alone, Antony reveals in a soliloquy that he intends to avenge the death of Caesar and is prepared to plunge Italy into civil war in order to accomplish it. A servant comes in with the news that Octavius, the young man whom Caesar had named as his heir, is only seven leagues outside Rome and intending to enter the city. Antony tells the servant to inform his master that it is too dangerous to be seen in Rome for the moment, for the city is in the hands of Caesar's enemies. But it is clear that Antony is calculating that Octavius will be a powerful ally if Antony can himself gain popularity and launch a counter-coup against Brutus and Cassius.

The next scene (III, ii) takes place in the Forum. Brutus sends Cassius to address some of the crowd in a neighbouring street, while he himself speaks to those already gathered in the Forum. Brutus tries to explain to his audience why he killed Caesar. Caesar's personal ambitions, he claims, would have led to restrictions in the liberties of Roman citizens. The crowd listen to him sympathetically and even want him to be the next Caesar, but Brutus asks them to listen courteously to Antony before they go. (He makes clear, however, that Antony is only speaking with the conspirators' permission.)

Once he has them to himself Antony sways the crowd to abandon their recent enthusiasm for Brutus and to believe that Caesar, far from threatening their freedom, had willed to each of them after his death a gift of money and the rights in perpetuity to treat his extensive gardens as their own. This news caps an argument which has involved an emphasis on Brutus' disloyalty to Caesar, who was his personal friend, and the display of Caesar's bloody, mutilated corpse. The crowd are incensed against the conspirators and Antony is pleased to let them loose, to burn and pillage and create the havoc which will enable him to gain political control of the city. The news is brought to him that Brutus and Cassius have fled, while Octavius and Lepidus have arrived and await Antony at Caesar's house.

In a nearby street (III, iii) we witness the lynching of an innocent citizen. A poet who happens, unluckily, to share the name of one of the conspirators (Cinna), is picked on by the mob and beaten to death. It is a shocking scene, which makes us despise the stupidity and violence of the people, but also the ambition and cynicism of Antony, who has deliberately worked them up into this frenzy and who hopes to make personal gain out of their brutality.

In the final scene in Rome (IV, i) the newly-formed Triumvirate – Antony, Octavius and Lepidus – are conducting a purge of their enemies, executing even their own close relatives. When Lepidus leaves the room, it soon becomes apparent that Antony has little time for him and is waiting for the opportunity to cut him out of the Triumvirate. Antony and Octavius are apprehensive that Brutus and Cassius are amassing an army to march against them.

We move from Rome to Sardis, in Asia Minor (IV, ii). Brutus and his troops meet Cassius and his troops, but the relations of the two generals are strained. Their reasons for killing Caesar had never been quite the same. They had disagreed about the wisdom of letting Antony live. But so long as the conspiracy was meeting with success Cassius always suppressed his differences with Brutus and they pulled together for the common good of their cause. Now, however, they have been driven out of Rome. Mutual irritation is weakening their friendship. They withdraw into Brutus' tent to discuss their differences.

Inside the tent the causes of their distrust are revealed (IV, iii). Brutus has condemned one Lucius Pella for taking bribes. Cassius knows the man and has written to Brutus, asking him to drop the charge, but Brutus has refused and Cassius feels slighted. Now, however, Brutus takes the opportunity to accuse Cassius himself of bribery. Cassius is riled and warns Brutus not to insult such an experienced soldier as himself. Brutus adds the further accusation that Cassius denied him money when he needed it to pay his troops. Cassius says that the man who carried the message between them misrepresented Cassius' reply.

Cassius claims to be heart-broken at this treatment by his brother-in-law. They are put into a better humour, however, by a poet who blunders into the tent and, in a couple of lines of doggerel verse, urges them to be good friends. Over a bowl of wine Brutus explains his ill-tempered mood as the expression of the grief he feels having heard that impatience at his absence and fear that Antony and Octavius were in a position to win the war have driven Portia to commit suicide. Messala and Titinius are called in, and Messala has news, not only of Portia's death, but also of the killings ordered by the Triumvirate. Brutus also has news. Antony and Octavius have brought an army to Philippi, in Macedonia. Cassius thinks they should wait for developments but Brutus overrules him, deciding that they should march up to Philippi and engage the enemy there.

Brutus is left alone with only the servant boy, Lucius, but he calls two of his officers into the tent to sleep. Soon only Brutus is awake, reading. The ghost of Caesar appears to him and says that it will appear once more, at Philippi. Brutus rouses the others and sends the message to Cassius that they must begin the march north.

Now we move to Philippi (V, i). Antony and Octavius can hardly believe their luck: rather than wait in the hills and hide their comparative weakness in numbers, Brutus and Cassius have rashly come into the open and are prepared to do battle. The four leaders meet before their armies and each pair hurls taunts at the other. Cassius is pessimistic, and he and Brutus privately shake hands in the knowledge that they may never meet again.

In the brief scene that follows (V, ii) battle is joined, and Brutus sends a message to Cassius on the opposite flank that he should push for victory.

Over on the other flank (V, iii), however, Cassius' troops are now in flight and he is attempting to restrain them. Retreating to a hill top, the short-sighted Cassius is unable to see what is happening to Brutus. He sends Titinius across to find out, but also asks Pindarus to keep watch on Titinius' movements and report what he can see. By a terrible irony, Pindarus mistakenly believes he can see Titinius fall into the hands of the enemy, for Titinius is surrounded by cheering troops. In the belief that they have lost the battle, Cassius proceeds to take his own life, using the very sword with which he had killed Caesar. But Titinius, far from being captured by the enemy, has in fact met up with Brutus' soldiers and has ridden back to tell Cassius that Brutus has just won an important victory. Luck has cruelly deserted the Republican side and the triumph of Antony and Octavius now seems inevitable. Titinius is so shaken by Cassius' suicide that he takes his own life out of respect for his general. Brutus then arrives, sees what tragedy has resulted from his victory, yet knows that he must launch another offensive later in the day.

In the penultimate scene (V, iv) we move to this second battle. Young Cato, fighting for the Republicans, falls. Lucilius is captured, deceiving the enemy into thinking that he is Brutus, but it is clear that the Republican cause is lost.

At another place on the battlefield (V, v) only Brutus and a few loyal troops are still resisting Antony and Octavius' army. Brutus knows that he will fall into the enemy's hands and has decided to follow Cassius' example and kill himself. He feels that Caesar's ghost is haunting him and that he must accept the punishment of death. He asks three of his soldiers in turn to assist him by holding the sword while he impales himself upon it. Each in turn refuses. All around him his troops are in flight. Finally, Strato agrees to hold the sword, Brutus runs on it and dies. The triumphant Antony and Octavius march in and find their enemy dead at their feet. Moved by this sight they pay tribute to the nobility of Brutus, denounce the other conspirators, and depart to celebrate their victory.

Scene by Scene Analysis

ACT I SCENE i

The play does not open with a scene involving Julius Caesar nor, indeed, any of the individual characters who are central to the action. Instead, we are introduced immediately to the common people of Rome, who have taken a day off work to line the streets and cheer Caesar as he passes by in a triumphal procession. They are not individuals but typical representatives of their trades (a Cobbler and a Carpenter speak). They show a disrespectful sense of humour, and, as we come to recognize more clearly later, political loyalties that are easily shifted by skilful public orators. This scene goes some way to establish this last fact, for the commoners are quickly persuaded to move away and clear the street by the verbal assaults of their leaders, Flavius and Marullus.

Flavius and Marullus are Tribunes of the People, that is, members of the Patrician class (the aristocracy) elected to represent the Plebeians (the ordinary people) in the government of Rome. It soon becomes clear, however, that Flavius and Marullus are no admirers of Julius Caesar. His triumphal procession celebrates his recent victory over the sons of the late Pompey the Great. Pompey had been the leader of one of the two political parties which had begun to struggle for power in Rome some thirty years earlier. Caesar had become the leader of the other party, and for a brief period he and Pompey had joined with a third politician, Crassus, to share the rule of Rome. This pact was known as the First Triumvirate. It had soon broken down and Pompey had emerged as sole ruler, but within a couple of years civil war had broken out between him and Caesar, and Caesar had eventually defeated Pompey in battle and taken over the rule of Rome himself.

Flavius and Marullus reveal themselves to have been supporters of Pompey in the civil war and they remind the crowd of the popularity Pompey had enjoyed before Caesar's victory three years ago.

The commoners are duly shamed by this accusation that they are fickle in their political loyalties (but later events demonstrate how very just the accusation is). At the same time we are given an insight into the power political leaders have over those who elect them. The Republic, we now know, is subject to the internal warring of opposing parties, those who once supported Pompey and those who now support Caesar.

ACT I SCENE ii

Caesar now enters at the head of his triumphal procession and he behaves, and is treated, as if he were a very special person. All his wishes are instantly obeyed. The deferential treatment he receives suggests either that he commands great respect or else that he is greatly feared. Nevertheless, the previous scene ended with a criticism of Caesar: Flavius' final words suggest that Caesar is puffed up with pride and wishes to 'soar above the view of men' (I, i, 74). Pride, they say, comes before a fall.

Caesar speaks Calphurnia's name and Casca calls immediately for silence. Caesar gives a series of instructions, telling Calphurnia where to stand, Antony where to run, and then commanding the procession to move forward. When he hears someone calling out from the crowd Caesar halts the procession as if on a whim, but having heard the Soothsayer's message he orders the procession to move on again. As Antony remarks, 'When Caesar says, "Do this", it is performed' (l. 10).

Caesar's speeches are for public consumption and it is even as if he were a member of his own public in a scene like this one. It is as if he were in awe of his own greatness when he announces, 'Caesar is turned to hear'. It may be that Caesar is such a majestic being that a hush always falls when he speaks or moves. But it may equally be that he is past his greatness and that his followers are cynically humouring him while holding him in contempt. We certainly learn later in this scene (ll. 214–91) that this is Casca's position.

Antony is one of the naked young men who are taking part in the fertility rites of the Lupercalia, and he is to touch Calphurnia as he runs past, to cure her barrenness. Caesar, by contrast, must seem old and sterile. Shakespeare also presents him as being deaf (l. 212). This detail reinforces the picture of an all too mortal being, but it also suggests that, for all that he listens to the Soothsayer in the crowd, he is tragically deaf to the Soothsayer's warning.

The scene is divided into four sections. After the opening section the stage is cleared of everyone except Cassius and Brutus. Immediately, Cassius begins to sound out his brother-in-law. Is Brutus going to watch Caesar's procession? No. Why not? He is inwardly at war with himself. Cassius is curious. He wishes to follow up the fact that Brutus is dissociating himself from Caesar. He claims to know Brutus better than Brutus knows himself. He tries to tempt Brutus to commit himself to a series of attitudes: that political life in Rome is intolerable; that Caesar makes it intolerable; that Caesar wishes to be a god; that Brutus has political ambitions; and that Caesar is thwarting them.

Brutus will not rise to any of these baits. But when there is a flourish of trumpets in the distance and the sound of a crowd shouting can be heard, Brutus lets slip the statement that Cassius has been angling for: 'I do fear the people/Choose Caesar for their king' (ll. 79–80). When Cassius asks eagerly if this means that Brutus would not want Caesar to be king, Brutus replies honestly, 'I would not, Cassius'. But he adds, 'yet I love him well'. Brutus always wishes to be on good terms with everybody. He knows that Caesar is his friend and loves him. But he is caught between quite contradictory impulses: his fear that Caesar might be persuaded to accept the crown comes into conflict with his loyalty to Caesar as a friend who trusts him.

Brutus attempts to convince Cassius that his attitude to Caesar is based on principle. He wishes to act, he says, for 'the general good', i.e. in the interests of all the Roman people. But he also wishes to behave honourably at all costs ('For let the gods so speed me as I love/The name of honour more than I fear death').

Cassius seizes on the word 'honour'. He thinks that the political success of a man like Caesar is a slur on the honour of men like Brutus and himself. He asks why Caesar's name should carry so much more weight in Roman politics than Brutus' name. He calls attention again to Brutus' name, in order to remind Brutus of his ancestor, the great Lucius Junius Brutus who rid Rome of its last king almost five hundred years ago. Brutus will dishonour the family name if he fails to follow his ancestor's example and save Rome from the threat of a man who is now aspiring to be king. Cassius has struck home. Brutus is tentative, but he concedes that 'What you would work me to, I have some aim' (l. 162).

When Caesar and his train re-enter, and we move into the third section of the scene, we look at Caesar in a new light. We know now that he has enemies, and we can see that envy and spite are not the only motives in those enemies' breasts. It is now less easy to respect Caesar. Cassius' picture of him as a physically enfeebled man is too vivid not to spoil any impression of grandeur which Caesar may himself entertain. We credit Caesar with the insight that leads him to distrust Cassius, especially when Antony is advising him that Cassius represents no danger (ll. 193–209). But he seems to have been shaken by some experience we have not witnessed. Where before we may have been impressed by Caesar's power and authority, he now seems vulnerable, even a little pathetic.

Shakespeare uses the fourth section of the scene, when Caesar has again gone out but Brutus has detained Casca to talk with him and Cassius, to do three things. First of all, he needs to inform us of what was going on off-stage during the second section. Casca provides us with an eye-witness account of some political showmanship in which Antony offered Caesar the crown and Caesar rejected it. Secondly, Shakespeare makes Casca's description of Caesar's behaviour so damning (implying, as it does, that Caesar is a complete hypocrite) that we can understand why Brutus might yield to the pressure to join Cassius' conspiracy. Thirdly, we cannot help attributing to Casca an irrational prejudice against Caesar. The effect is to make us distrust both Caesar and those who oppose him with the greatest intensity. We begin to realize that this is not going to be one of those stories in which the characters are either 'good' or 'bad', heroes or villains.

Casca's opinion is that the public gesture of Antony offering the crown and Caesar ostentatiously refusing it was a put-up job. Caesar rejected the crown because he knew that such a gesture would please the 'tag-rag people' (l. 256). In fact, so Casca would have us believe, Caesar has every wish to accept the crown but is gradually building his public support by pretending to be modest and apprehensive about taking such a momentous step.

This interpretation by Casca may not be accurate but it is plausible. The scorn he goes on to direct at Caesar is vicious. He says he wanted to laugh when Caesar fell down in an epileptic fit. He finds the indignity of it very funny, because Caesar is so conscious of maintaining a dignified image in public. (This impulse to laugh may also be prompted by what Casca has aleady called the 'foolery' of Caesar's undignified piece of blatant showmanship.) He also finds it ironical that Caesar should have been courting the common people but then have been overcome by their 'stinking breath'. We may find another irony in it too, when we look back on this scene after the assassination of Caesar (III, i), for when he dies Caesar falls again to the ground, hacked down in a bloody heap by the swords of these three men, Casca, Cassius and Brutus.

That is a chilling thought. But Casca now adds in his own bit of chilling information: Marullus and Flavius, the Tribunes from Act I Scene i, have been 'put to silence'. Caesar may be vain and past his prime, and men may laugh at him, but he wields terrifying power.

Casca goes, but Cassius arranges to dine with him next day. When Brutus also leaves, he suggests to Cassius that they should also meet on the following day. The discontent encouraged by Cassius is not going to be allowed to settle.

Left alone, Cassius reveals for us just how unscrupulous he is prepared to be. It is his intention to take advantage, not only of Brutus' fear that Caesar really wants to be king, but also of Brutus' slight touch of vanity – the idea that Rome holds a great opinion of his name. Caesar may be thinking that, after his success with the crowd, he is strong and politically secure, but Cassius intends to 'shake him' (l. 319). And as he leaves the stage, the universe itself seems to have been listening, for the next lines of the play are accompanied by thunder in the heavens and earthquakes under foot.

ACT I SCENE iii

Cicero and Casca meet in the street. A first reading suggests that Cicero, the famous orator, whose knowledge of Greek was worthy of Casca's comment in the previous scene (I, ii, 276), is introduced here merely to allow Casca the opportunity to describe the terrifying storm which is raging during the scene. But the two men have different responses to the storm, and the response of Cassius, who enters later in the scene, is different again. Shakespeare is interested in these different responses, for they represent quite different beliefs about the relationship men have to the universe in which they live.

For Casca, the storm is a portent, a sign from the gods. He is breathless and staring, frightened and overawed by what he has seen: fire falling from the sky; a slave whose hand burnt brilliantly but without any physical effect on the hand itself; tales of men covered in fire walking the streets. There are other prodigies, too: a lion harmlessly wandering near the Capitol, an owl hooting and shrieking in the market-place at midday. And, all the time, lightning is flashing and thunder crashing and booming.

Casca believes that the gods are using these extraordinary events to warn mankind. But he cannot work out what the warning is. Cicero, on the other hand, is less clear whether or not the storm is any more than bad weather. He remains uncommitted over this issue, just as he is to remain uncommitted over the conspiracy to kill Caesar (II, i, 141–53). Cicero holds no very clear views, but makes an important point here:

> . . . *men may construe things after their fashion,*
> *Clean from the purpose of the things themselves.*

(ll. 34–5)

Men see things as they want to see them, and sometimes entirely misinterpret them. Cassius, who enters now, is to die as the result of a tragic misunderstanding in the last act of the play (V, iii, 32ff.), and the action of the play as a whole frequently turns upon disagreements between characters as to the correct interpretation of events.

Cassius is quite fearless of the stormy night. Indeed, he is positively attracted to it, challenging the heavens to harm him. In the previous scene Cassius told Brutus that men are not totally ruled by the stars, for 'Men at some time are masters of their fates' (I, ii, 138). Here he seems more emphatic in his faith that there are no such things as omens, that the gods do not control our lives and that we, being free agents, must control them ourselves. He even makes a joke out of Casca's fear that the storm represents the anger of the gods, and claims that if it is a comment on anything the storm must be telling us that Caesar has grown 'prodigious' and 'fearful'. Caesar, he suggests, is a man so swollen with pride that he thinks himself above nature, a man who 'thunders, lightens, opens graves, and roars/As doth the lion in the Capitol' (ll. 74–5).

The effect of the storm on Cassius is to fill him with the boldness to become master of his fate, to plot the downfall of Caesar and, to this end, to draw Brutus into a conspiracy. Cassius is fearless because he reckons he has 'the strength of spirit', not only to break free from what he considers the prison of Caesar's rule but, if he fails, to determine his own life by ending it in suicide. He explains later in the play that he has always been a follower of the philosophy of Epicurus (V, i, 76), who emphasized man's freedom of action in a world to which the gods were indifferent. But in this reference to suicide Cassius seems to be drawing on Stoicism, a philosophy which Brutus tries to live by (IV, iii, 143–4). Stoicism is more fatalistic than Epicureanism, denying man's freedom except in so far as he can adapt his mind to accept the inevitability of his fate. But, for the Stoic, the act of taking one's own life, when the alternative is dishonour, is the ultimate freedom.

Cassius is careful not to speak too directly about his hatred of Caesar, at least not at first. But Casca has already expressed his hatred in the previous scene and when Casca refers to the rumour that it is Caesar's intention to accept the crown next day in the Capitol Cassius makes plain that he is prepared to forestall such a move by force. On this day of the Lupercal (the festival of the shepherd) Cassius calls his fellow Romans sheep, weakly exposing themselves to the imminent tyranny of the wolf, Caesar. Casca reassures Cassius that he will join the conspiracy, and immediately there enters another conspirator, Cinna, with news of still others – Metellus Cimber, Decius Brutus and

Trebonius – all meeting at Pompey's Porch. Cassius sends him off to deliver bogus letters to Brutus, so that he will be misled into believing that a whole range of citizens is looking to him to assassinate Caesar.

By the end of the scene Cassius and Casca are confident that it is but a few hours before Brutus will join them and thereby ensure them the support of his great personal following among the Roman people.

ACT II SCENE i

So far we have been out in the streets and public places of Rome. Now we enter a man's private home. Brutus is alone in his garden in the middle of the night, unable to sleep and calling his servant boy to bring him a taper so that he can read in his study. Brutus' insomnia derives from his thoughts, and in a soliloquy he reveals the pattern of these thoughts. He begins 'It must be by his death' (l. 10). We are not told what 'It' refers to, nor, at least at first, whose death he is imagining. We have come in on the middle of something. These thoughts, this internal argument, is clearly going round and round in Brutus' brain. We have to pick up the threads and infer that 'It' means something like 'The solution to my fear that Caesar intends to be crowned king of Rome', and that the solution is assassination. In other words, Brutus' private deliberations have brought him to the point that Cassius has just prophesied he will reach, a willingness to join a conspiracy against Caesar's life.

Brutus' argument tells us a great deal about the kind of man he is. He knows that two principles are at war – personal cause and general cause, as he calls them. He has no personal motive for killing Caesar, he will be doing it for the general cause, the good of Rome. Equally, these two terms 'personal' and 'general' nicely describe another pair of principles. Caesar's personal nature is known to be honourable and rational, but the general nature of Mankind is that power corrupts. Brutus argues that, once crowned and therefore given absolute power, Caesar will be beyond the power of anyone else to check or restrain him. Nothing could stop him turning into a tyrant.

Then, lest he may, prevent.   (l. 28)

The argument depends on two acts of judgement by Brutus. One is that there is force in the axiom that power corrupts and absolute power corrupts absolutely. The other is the assumption that 'He would be crowned' (l. 12). Our knowledge of Caesar does not permit us to say this with the same confidence that Brutus says it. We have only second-hand accounts of the off-stage events in Act I Scene ii when Caesar thrice refused the proffered crown. Was Caesar's response genuine or assumed? Even if he genuinely did not want to be king would Caesar give in to pressure from supporters like Antony? And if Caesar really wants the crown is he only manipulating public sympathy by seeming to resist absolute power? Brutus, being a close friend of Caesar, is in a position to know Caesar's likely principles and desires. But can anyone know even his friends' inner lives? (As we shall see later, Caesar is astonished that Brutus of all people should be his assassin.)

Brutus is decided: Caesar must be stopped, for the danger of letting him go further is too immense to be permitted. The danger, of course, is to Rome. And Brutus is now brought a letter, one of those forgeries planted by Cinna on Cassius' behalf. The night sky is so full of the fiery apparitions described in Act I Scene iii that Brutus can read the letter as he stands out in his garden. The letter speaks of Brutus as being asleep (ironically, Brutus is unable to sleep!), implying that he is ignoring the threat to Rome which Caesar poses. Shakespeare reminds us at this moment that we are in the early hours of 15 March. The letter exhorts Brutus to 'strike', that is, to kill Caesar. The 15 March is the Ides of March, the date the Soothsayer warned Caesar of.

The scene is in four sections, and the first, being the presentation of Brutus in his isolation and in the anxious thrall of his thoughts about Caesar, is now over. A knock at the door heralds the entry of Cassius and the other conspirators. Dawn is breaking on this fateful day as they shake Brutus' hand and allow him gradually to take control of their enterprise. He will not let them swear an oath of commitment to the good of Rome. To swear such an oath demeans their enterprise because it implies that without an oath they will not be faithful to the cause. He rejects their opinion that Cicero should be asked to join. He rejects Cassius' suggestion that Antony be killed along with Caesar. In doing this Brutus reveals not only his inept judgement ('for Mark Antony, think not of him;/For he can do no more than Caesar's arm/When Caesar's head is off', ll. 181–3), sparing the man who will eventually overthrow Brutus and Cassius, once they have achieved power. He also exhibits his ability to idealize things to a morally dangerous degree. In his imagination the killing of Caesar will not be an act of murder at all. It will lack any brutality, any cruelty, any physical dimension. It will not be done out of passion; it will be spiritual and purifying.

> *Let us be sacrificers, but not butchers, Caius.*
> . . .
> *Let's carve him as a dish fit for the gods,*
> *Not hew him as a carcass fit for hounds.*
> . . .
> *We shall be called purgers, not murderers.*
>
> (ll. 166, 173–4, 180)

Brutus' brain transforms the act of murder into the necessary sacrifice of his friend for the common good, for the traditions of Rome, and for the divine ideal of Liberty.

But will Caesar be there at the Capitol today? The Soothsayer's prophecy and the strange portents of the night might frighten him away. Decius claims to know Caesar's character and is confident that he will be there. Caesar, he says, is easily swayed by flattery.

> *But when I tell him he hates flatterers,*
> *He says he does, being then most flatterèd.*   (ll. 207–8)

If Decius says the right things to him Caesar will set out for the Capitol at eight a.m.

Now we move into the third section. It is three a.m. and we have an opportunity to observe Brutus as he faces private, as opposed to public, problems. Lucius is asleep. Portia enters and Brutus asks her why she is up so early. She throws the question back at him and complains that he has been behaving unnaturally for some days – he has been restless, touchy, preoccupied, off his food. She appeals to him, if he loves her, to tell her what is worrying him. She reminds him that she is the daughter of Cato the Stoic and the supporter of Pompey, and that she has inherited from him a belief in the importance of loyalty to friends and the capacity to endure physical pain (she shows him a self-inflicted wound in her thigh which she has borne without giving in to the pain). Surely she will honour any secrets Brutus has to tell her? But before he can answer there is a knock at the door and a sick man with his head muffled up in a cloth for warmth is ushered in.

In the brief fourth section of the scene this man, Caius Ligarius, a former supporter of Pompey, sounds out Brutus over his attitude to Caesar. When he hears that Brutus is part of the conspiracy to overthrow Caesar, Ligarius feels instantly recovered from his illness, calls Brutus 'Soul of Rome' and praises him as the honourable descendant of the famous Junius Brutus, who liberated Rome from the Tyrants. Thunder can be heard as the two men set out for the Capitol.

ACT II SCENE ii

This is a second domestic scene, this time in Caesar's house. He is in his night-gown rather than his public finery. Like Brutus he has had a disturbed night, and the thunder and lightning are still in the background. In this scene, too, the public man is under attack from his wife. Calphurnia has had a dream that Caesar's statue has been spouting blood. We learn of more prodigies observed in the streets of Rome (ghosts, a drizzle of blood over the Capitol, a lioness giving birth in the street). Calphurnia interprets these signs and her dream as prophetic of her husband's death.

Caesar has ordered priests to sacrifice an animal to the gods and read the entrails. Report comes that this has been performed and the amazing discovery made that the animal had no heart. Calphurnia is terrified (if Rome loses its heart, that must be Caesar). Caesar argues that the gods are challenging him to prove that he has a heart, i.e. the courage to go to the Capitol as he had arranged. Nevertheless Calphurnia prevails and Caesar asks Decius Brutus, when he arrives, to inform the Senators that he will not be attending the Senate House after all. Caesar will not send the lie that he is unable to attend: a falsehood would dishonour him. On the other hand he is not afraid to attend and would be dishonoured if Decius suggested such a thing to the Senate. To say he *will* not come emphasizes his own will, his choosing his destiny, and he likes that idea. On the other hand he feels obliged to tell Decius that the real reason is Calphurnia's fear, prompted by a dream that his statue was spouting blood and that Romans were bathing their hands in the blood and smiling. Once again we are reminded that it is impossible to know how to interpret something like a dream. To Calphurnia this dream prophesies Caesar's death. Decius tells Caesar that it prophesies the gratitude of future Romans to Caesar for his benevolent life. He claims that Caesar will be humiliated if the news comes that Calphurnia's dreams are enough to dissuade Caesar from attending the Senate.

Perhaps the most interesting thing that Decius says here is that 'The Senate have concluded/To give this day a crown to mighty Caesar' (ll. 93–4). It may or may not be true. Decius is doing what he told the conspirators he could do, flattering and tempting Caesar into attending the Senate. And Caesar decides to come. So we can conclude, if we want to, that Brutus was right, and Caesar does intend to accept the crown.

At any rate, Caesar's susceptibility to flattery is confirmed. And Caesar is revealed as being a man who quickly changes his mind, yet boasts he is constant in his purpose. Before he can change his mind again Brutus leads in a group of Senators (we know them to be conspirators) to accompany Caesar to the Capitol. It is now eight a.m. The disturbed night is over and the new day begun. But another man who has probably slept little now enters – Antony 'that revels long a-nights' (l. 116). Antony joins the group of flatterers as they leave the house of Caesar, the man who leads them to the scene of what he believes will be his greatest triumph.

ACT II SCENE iii

A single figure comes on to the stage and reads out a letter he intends giving to Caesar as he passes on the way to the Capitol. Artemidorus raises the issue of Caesar's immortality: 'If thou beest not immortal, look about you' (ll. 6–7). We know he is not immortal. To us he has appeared all too human. But are there Romans who are almost convinced that Caesar is divine? And is Caesar himself under such an impression?

Artemidorus names each of the conspirators in order, beginning with Brutus. He bids Caesar beware. Shakespeare seems to want to make sure that we do not forget the names of the men who are prepared to assassinate the famous Dictator. At II, i, 94–6 Brutus shook their hands in turn when they came to his house in the night. And at III, i, 184–9 Antony will shake their hands in the Capitol, rehearsing the names of those who will by then have carried out the assassination.

ACT II SCENE iv

Portia is struggling with the dangerous information she now has. We can only assume that Brutus has confided in her or else that she has put two and two together and realized that her husband is part of a conspiracy to kill Caesar. She is bursting to make this news public but she is sworn to silence. Her constancy is at stake, just as, in a different way, Caesar thought his constancy was at stake. She urges Lucius to run to the Capitol and report back what he witnesses there. But before he can go a Soothsayer enters, on *his* way to the Capitol where, like Artemidorus, he intends to warn Caesar of the danger he is in. Thus, in a few lines, Shakespeare presents those who wish to protect Caesar, and Portia, who secretly calls on the gods to speed her husband in his enterprise. This tension is added to by Shakespeare's insistence that we note how time is passing and the moment of the assassination is approaching. In Act II Scene i we were told it was 15 March, it was three a.m., it was day-break. In Act II Scene ii it came to be eight a.m. Now it is nine a.m. and a throng of Senators, Praetors and common suitors are at Caesar's heels as he passes through the narrow streets to the Senate House.

ACT III SCENE i

This big public scene opens with a flurry of activity. Caesar notices the Soothsayer in the crowd and reminds him jocularly that today is the Ides of March. The Soothsayer replies that the Ides are not yet over. A conspirator vies with a genuine well-wisher for Caesar's attention. Caesar dismisses both.

The nervousness of the conspirators is further expressed in Cassius' reaction to the remark of Popilius Lena, who cryptically wishes his 'enterprise' well. We know from the previous scene that Brutus may have told his wife about the conspiracy. All this re-arouses our excitement and anticipation. Brutus urges Cassius to be 'constant' – that is, calm, composed, resolute. Mark Antony, whom we have been led to regard as Caesar's one ally, is drawn away on a pretext. Caesar is alone at the mercy of his enemies.

Metellus Cimber kneels before him, thus emphasizing in visual terms the respect due to Caesar but, at the same time, the hypocrisy of the conspirators. Caesar shows no pity for Metellus' brother, Publius, when he is asked to repeal his banishment. Is this refusal the 'abuse of greatness . . . when it disjoins/Remorse from power' (these words were uttered by Brutus in his garden soliloquy at II, i, 18–19), or does it demonstrate that Caesar is what he claims to be, consistent in his judgements?

Brutus and Cassius, and then Cinna and Decius, drop to their knees alongside Metellus and add their voices to his in support of Publius' pardon. Caesar proclaims that he will not yield: 'I am constant as the northern star' (l. 60). By giving him this kind of arrogance Shakespeare must deprive Caesar of some of our sympathy. But his murder follows immediately, and it is so brutal and bloody, and Caesar is so horrified to find that his friend, Brutus, is treacherous enough to be one of the killers, that our sympathy is immediately re-awakened.

Caesar has collapsed at the base of Pompey's statue, as if Pompey had taken his revenge, and the conspirators cry out that 'Tyranny is dead!' (l. 78). Grand ideas about justice and liberty are in the air, but blood is on the ground, and blood is messy and stinks. Some of the conspirators realize that their own lives are now in danger, but Brutus is so caught up by ideas that he calls out to those witnesses who have not run away in terror that they have been privileged to see a moral act. He imagines future generations reverently re-enacting this drama and drawing moral lessons from it. The irony is that the lessons drawn are frequently different from those that Brutus has in mind.

Brutus seems not to see the blood as real blood at all. For him it is a symbol of a solemn act of purification, the purification of Rome. The impurity in the government of Rome was Caesar's ambition, and now that he is dead the threat to Rome is over. He therefore persuades his fellow conspirators to smear Caesar's blood all over their hands and forearms, as if they had taken part in an act of ritual sacrifice. He is proud of the blood on his hands, for he does not see it as a sign of murder. He is a freedom fighter, not a criminal.

But if Brutus is to be regarded as a political activist there is a fatal gap in his political strategy. Brutus makes no mention of any plan he has for the government of Rome, once Caesar is no longer there in charge. It is as if the removal of Caesar were the only issue. But how long will freedom last in the confusion and power vacuum that is bound to follow the assassination? Brutus' mind has been preoccupied with the assassination as an event in the future. Now it has happened it is already receding into the past. We have come to a turning point in the play. And the next event heralds the new future, a future which, far from safeguarding the peace and political stability of Rome, brings wide-scale destruction and the deaths of virtually every character we have so far encountered.

I say *virtually* every character, for one character survives and prospers, and that is Mark Antony. And the next event is the arrival of Antony's servant announcing Antony's wish to be allowed to enter and talk to the conspirators. Antony has not spoken since Act I Scene 2 but he dominates the rest of this scene and the next, and he does so not only because he is a great orator and strategist but also because he understands the situation created by Caesar's assassination. He understands the characters of the conspirators, the character of the Roman mob, and the character of those whom he intends to make his political allies.

His servant prostrates himself before Brutus. We recall the conspirators kneeling before Caesar at the beginning of the scene. Caesar had the power, and Brutus has it now.

Antony's message is that he honoured Caesar and that he honours Brutus. ('Honour' is a word Antony is going to use skilfully in the next scene when he addresses the crowd in the Forum.) Brutus sends back the message that, if he comes to talk with the conspirators, Antony will discover why they have killed Caesar. Cassius senses that Antony is someone they should fear, but he lets Brutus go ahead.

When Antony enters, his first words are not to the conspirators but to the dead Caesar. Even when he speaks to them he devotes his speech to an act of proud defiance by identifying with Caesar. In his reply Brutus argues that, for all its apparent cruelty, the killing was done out of pity – pity, not for Caesar, but for the Roman people who were threatened with a tyrant's rule. And while Brutus is persisting in his attempt to give the assassination a theoretical justification, Cassius attempts to stave off danger by making Antony a vague offer of a political partnership.

But Antony embarks on an extraordinary charade. He ritually shakes each of the assassins by the hand. But he makes clear, by describing the murder as the hunting of a hart, that he will not accept Brutus' view of the killing. By shaking each bloody hand Antony covers his own hand in blood, as if he, too, had joined in Brutus' symbolic ritual and purified the deed. But Antony's gesture is a deliberate cheat. The blood on his hand is the blood of the man whose death he means to avenge, and any further bloodshed will be a matter of Antony killing the conspirators.

For the moment, however, Antony is lulling Brutus into a false sense of security. He asks to be allowed to speak over Caesar's corpse in a public funeral. Brutus instantly agrees, ignoring Cassius' shrewd warning about Antony's power to move an audience. Antony agrees to speak only after Brutus has himself delivered a funeral oration. Brutus is confident that the public will appreciate the magnanimity with which Antony is being treated, and he and the other conspirators leave the stage.

Now that he is alone Antony's true feelings burst out: he will avenge 'the noblest man/That ever livèd' (ll. 256–7); he prophesies that there will be a pitiless civil war. A servant of Octavius Caesar comes with the news that his master is approaching Rome. Antony sends back a message that Octavius should wait a little. But he knows, and we know, that already there is significant opposition to Brutus' coup, and that there is now the possibility of a counter-coup.

ACT III SCENE ii

Brutus and Cassius each take a section of the crowd and address it. We see and hear only Brutus, and soon forget about Cassius and his half of the crowd, but Shakespeare suggests the size of the politicians' problems (and power) by establishing that a similar scene is taking place in the next street.

Brutus goes up into the pulpit and addresses the crowd. He appeals to them as 'Romans' before all else, and this is in keeping with his reasons for joining the conspiracy. He builds his own case on the concept of 'honour', and this too is in keeping with his reasons for joining the conspiracy.

His speech to the people is honest and consistent with all his thinking and arguing throughout the play. He has no thought of deceiving them. But his speech is nevertheless a shrewd, skilful piece of rhetoric. He speaks calmly and reasonably but he has created a kind of hysteria in the crowd by the time he has finished. The speech may be in prose, but its rhythmic patterning, the balancing out of similar phrases, and the repetition of the word 'love' or the phrase 'for him have I offended' are as contrived and emotive in their cumulative effect as any passage of poetry.

Brutus builds up a picture of what it means to be a true Roman: one who loves his country and freedom, and who hates rude slavery and the base status of bondman. By the end, having argued that Caesar's ambition made him the enemy of Rome, Brutus is implying that it is rude and base to protest at the killing of Caesar. He ends by offering his life for his country. It is all very emotional, and one recalls Casca's description of Caesar offering his life to the crowd.

Brutus does not respond to the crowd's delirious adulation. He honours his promise to Antony, but emphasizes, as he leaves the pulpit and the stage, that Antony will be speaking 'by our permission'. By entrusting the crowd to Antony Brutus makes a quite fatal error of judgement. His naive belief that Antony will honour the spirit of their agreement loses Brutus all his power in Rome.

Antony draws all attention away from Brutus, even before he has finished speaking, by entering with the body of Caesar. In theatrical language he can be said to 'up-stage' Brutus. He may not have been present during Brutus' speech but he shapes his own speech to complement it and, finally, to destroy all the effects Brutus had so brilliantly achieved.

Brutus had appealed to his audience's civic pride and also to its sense of logic. Antony works to undermine Brutus' grand ideas and words, using an actor's control over his audience's emotions. Where Brutus had begun with the word 'Romans' Antony chooses to begin with 'Friends'. He quickly creates the feeling that he and the crowd, and the dead Caesar too, all make up a close group of friends. He flatters them, but he is also prepared to be angry with them, to shame them by weeping over the corpse and to castigate them for withholding their tears.

Having established the idea of this body of friends, he begins to open up a split between them and the other group, the conspirators. And he does this by encouraging in them a cynicism about Brutus. Brutus had presented himself to them as a man of *honour*. Antony reminds them of this. And he goes on reminding them, until the idea comes to sound hollow. Each time we hear 'And Brutus is an honourable man' the case for Brutus' honour is weakened. And by the time Antony has finished, 'honour' has become a term of mockery. Brutus had required Antony not to attack the conspirators in his speech. By using a term of praise Antony has kept to the bargain, while subtly breaking it.

Now Antony produces a document and holds it up to the crowd, tempting them with its contents. It is, he claims, Caesar's will, a rich legacy he has left to the people of Rome. He pretends that he will not read it. If he were to, it would wrong 'the honourable men/Whose daggers have stabbed Caesar' (ll. 152–3). 'Honourable men!', his audience cries out, 'villains, murderers!' Greed has won them to the view that Brutus and Cassius would have cheated them of their inheritance. Antony has become their saviour.

Antony takes immediate advantage of this surge of self-interest:

> *You will compel me then to read the will?*
> *Then make a ring about the corpse of Caesar,*
> *And let me show you him that made the will.*
> *Shall I descend?*   (ll. 158–61)

By descending to the level of the crowd Antony triumphs over Brutus. Caesar had swooned when he got close to them; Brutus had stayed aloft in the pulpit; but Antony enters their ring and draws us all, Romans and theatre audience alike, into his intimate revelation of the bloody treason done to Caesar.

He can drop all pretence now. The conspirators acted out of envy and ingratitude, and when Caesar fell 'Then I, and you, and all of us fell down'. Now the crowd are weeping with him.

And, next, they are transformed into avengers. 'Revenge! About! Seek! Burn! Fire! Kill! Slay!' Antony can still control them if he wishes. He calls them back, pointing out that they have forgotten Caesar's will. But when he lets them go again, they are intent on destroying *anything*, and Antony has unleashed a force which effectively sweeps him to power.

The mood is frightening enough, but when Antony stops calling them 'you' and refers cynically to 'them' instead, we in the audience are suddenly shocked and shamed. We had been drawn into his conspiracy. We had been part of the crowd, listening to Antony with a mixture of awe and delight at the brilliance of his rhetoric and theatrical skill. When we see the next scene, we are sick with the crowd, sick with Antony, and sick with ourselves.

ACT III SCENE iii

The scene of Caesar's assassination is a brutal one, but, if anything, this little scene is more terrible still. What both alleviates and yet intensifies its terrible nature is the grotesque comedy of the circumstances in which Cinna the Poet is lynched by the mob whom Antony has let loose on Rome.

Like Calphurnia, Cinna dreamt during the night – of feasting with Caesar. What might have seemed like a privilege and honour now frightens him, and yet he comes out into the streets as if still in a dream-state. The Plebeians surround him demanding to know his identity, taunting and threatening him. When he declares he is a friend to Caesar they nevertheless persist in their questioning. When he says his name is Cinna they assume he is Cinna the conspirator and cry out 'Tear him to pieces!' (l. 28). When he protests that they have got the wrong Cinna, that he is a poet and not a politician, they ignore the distinction: 'It is no matter; his name's Cinna' (l. 33). And they proceed to beat him up and probably kill him.

The Plebeians are hell-bent on destruction, they don't mind killing and it doesn't seem to matter who gets killed. Cinna is torn to pieces, just as a poet tears up a bad poem. The mob rush out determined to destroy the houses belonging to all the conspirators – and once again the names of the conspirators are listed, so that the scene ends with these names ringing in our ears: 'To Brutus', to Cassius'; burn all! Some to Decius' house, and some to Casca's; some to Ligarius'.' (ll. 36–8)

ACT IV SCENE i

This is another unpleasant scene. The raging passion of the mob, which leads them to blood lust and the desire to fire the city, is now replaced suddenly by the cold-hearted ruthlessness of those who have profited by the outburst of anarchy. In a play which is so interested in the concept of honour, the behaviour of Antony here seems less than honourable. Brutus and Cassius have fled Rome, and in their place the Second Triumvirate (the name used by historians to refer to the joint rule of Antony, Octavius and Lepidus) have power. Antony and Octavius are in committee with Lepidus, reading a list. They are purging Rome of those who led the coup which toppled Caesar. They are even trading their own relations as the number of those condemned grows larger.

> OCTAVIUS *Your brother too must die; consent you, Lepidus?*
> LEPIDUS *I do consent ...*
> *Upon condition Publius shall not live,*
> *Who is your sister's son, Mark Antony.*
> ANTONY *He shall not live. Look, with a spot I damn him.*
>
> (ll. 2–6)

Then Antony sends Lepidus out of the room to find another sheet of paper, Caesar's will, and once he is gone Antony sneers at him behind his back, commenting that he is only fit to be sent about on errands. He explains to Octavius, whose youth and inexperience he patronizes, that Lepidus is useful at this stage, for he shoulders some of the blame for drawing up the death list. But Antony despises him as lacking all initiative and originality of thought. It is clear that Lepidus' days are numbered. The new set of conspirators are beginning to fall out, and the Triumvirate will never last. Octavius is apprehensive that they are surrounded by enemies and Antony advises that they build up their army to answer any attack which the exiled Brutus and Cassius might launch on Rome.

ACT IV SCENE ii

The whole of the play up to this point has been set in Rome. Now, we switch to a new location, Sardis (which is in Asia Minor).

This is the meeting of the two armies in exile. Titinius and Pindarus, representing Cassius, are informed by Brutus that he is less than happy with Cassius, and Lucilius confides to Brutus that Cassius is less friendly than he has been. When he enters, Cassius' first words to Brutus are a blunt reproach, an entirely new tone in their relationship – 'Most noble brother, you have done me wrong' (l. 37). He calls him brother because they are not only leaders of the conspiracy but brothers-in-law as well. Because Brutus' response is to urge Cassius to come into the privacy of his tent, Shakespeare ensures that the quarrel which ensues is seen by us as a private feud between brothers-in-law as well as the falling out of political and military leaders. But in so far as it is the latter we are bound to draw the parallel with the signs of a rift opening up in the Triumvirate during the preceding scene. Shakespeare is interested in the tensions involved in all political groupings where strong individuals are forced to compromise their ambitions and ideals for the good of certain ends they have in common. Such groupings are shown to be threatened by the temperaments of those who make them up, by the changing political situation, and by the passage of time and the intervention of chance.

ACT IV SCENE iii

Brutus has heard that Portia is dead. She has killed herself by swallowing fire, driven mad by worry at the absence of Brutus and the news that Antony and Octavius are leading a strong army against him. Brutus is depressed, irritable, and possibly feeling guilty too.

Yet Shakespeare deliberately keeps the news of Portia's death from us for the moment, and Cassius knows nothing of it either. In our ignorance, therefore, we watch an apparent deterioration in the behaviour of Brutus, who has seemed so noble until this scene. When we later learn of his private grief we are forced to recognize how hard it is for a man to match the ideal standards that Brutus expects all men, including himself, to live up to.

As soon as they enter the tent Cassius explains the cause of *his* annoyance. Lucius Pella has been publicly disgraced by Brutus for taking bribes in Sardis and Cassius' letters pleading leniency out of loyalty to Lucius Pella have been brushed aside. Cassius is angry that Brutus should ignore his opinions and also that Brutus should take so seriously a minor offence when they are facing a military crisis. But Brutus' rejoinder is to accuse Cassius of being susceptible to bribery himself. He tells Cassius that they killed Caesar in the name of justice (a new idea), and that Caesar had given his protection to robbers (a piece of information Shakespeare has made no reference to before this moment). Brutus implies that Cassius is a robber and unworthy of having joined the honourable cause of assassinating Caesar.

Cassius' response is to warn Brutus to be careful and not to impugn the honour of a soldier of superior experience and ability in man-management. They fall to an undignified quarrelling which takes the form of abuse ('Away, slight man!', 'madman'), hair-splitting ('I said an elder soldier, not a better;/Did I say better?') and infantile assertions and counter-assertions:

> BRUTUS   *Go to! You are not Cassius.*
> CASSIUS *I am.*
> BRUTUS *I say you are not.*   (ll. 32–4)

Brutus then introduces a second complaint against Cassius – that he meanly refused him money to pay his army. Two interesting features arise. Brutus is self-righteously boastful of his own virtue:

> *... I can raise no money by vile means;*
> *By heaven, I had rather coin my heart,*
> *And drop my blood for drachmas, than to wring*
> *From the hard hands of peasants their vile trash*
> *By any indirection.*   (ll. 71–5)

This is an unattractive side to Brutus, who has previously seemed so virtuous, if misguided. On the other hand, whatever the truth of

Brutus' accusations, Cassius appears the more sympathetic of the two, wounded that his friend (ll. 85, 89) should have turned on him so vindictively and 'rived' his heart (l. 84). Still, Cassius' pain is somewhat overplayed, as he calls on Brutus to stab him in the breast if he thinks so badly of him. Brutus' anger is over, however, and he apologizes for his outburst. Cassius apologizes for his temper. They are reconciled.

There follows a curious interlude in which a poet (the second in the play, incidentally) gate-crashes the generals' private meeting and advises them to

> *Love and be friends, as two such men should be;*
> *For I have seen more years, I'm sure, than ye.*   (ll. 129–30)

The poet is bustled out, Brutus dismissing him on the grounds that poetry is out of place in war, Cassius scorning the quality of his rhyming couplet. If this interlude has any purpose it is to seal the reconciliation of the generals and to lighten the mood, while reminding us that very serious matters are afoot.

Brutus calls for wine so that Cassius can drink with him in friendship. Then he begins to explain that his anger has deeper causes than he had been admitting: he has been weighed down with grief because his wife, Portia, is dead. She missed him and was afraid of Antony and Octavius' growing strength so she went out of her mind and committed suicide. Cassius is aghast, but Brutus asks him to mention it no more.

Portia had been proud of her fortitude and constancy of purpose (II, i, 294–302). Her father, Cato, was a famous follower of the philosophy of Stoicism, which preached that suffering should be endured and self-control recognized as a major virtue. Yet we saw her nervous anxiety on the day of the assassination (II, iv). It is a cruel irony that she should have killed herself like Cato, but that it should have resulted not from Stoic pride in demonstrating control over events but from a desperate loss of control. The issue of Stoicism is further developed in this scene. When Cassius is told that Brutus is grieving over something, his immediate response is to remind Brutus that he prides himself on the self-control preached by the Stoics:

> *Of your philosophy you make no use,*
> *If you give place to accidental evils.*   (ll. 143–4)

Brutus seems to be in control of his feelings now, but Cassius is still brooding over Portia's death when Titinius and Messala have been called into the tent to discuss the military situation. The news is that Antony and Octavius are leading a big army towards Philippi, having executed between seventy and a hundred Senators, including Cicero.

Brutus is now seen receiving the news of Portia's death from Messala. All he says in response is

> *Why, farewell, Portia. We must die, Messala.*
> *With meditating that she must die once,*
> *I have the patience to endure it now.*   (ll. 188–90)

This is Stoical. The philosophical observation that all of us die has led Brutus into acceptance of Portia's death whenever it should occur. There is a contrast between this unmoved reaction and the Brutus who explained his ill-temper earlier in the scene by referring to his grief over Portia's death. Brutus has now regained sufficient self-control to behave before Messala with the dignity that temporarily deserted him in the undignified quarrel with Cassius.

Brutus changes the subject to the issue of the next step they ought to take in the war. Cassius advises waiting for Antony and Lepidus to make the first move. Brutus, however, believes that their strength and support from others are at their height and that delay will only weaken their position. Cassius agrees to follow Brutus' opinion. As always the outcome is a disaster.

They decide to stop talking and turn in for the night. Cassius, Titinius and Messala leave. Brutus asks his servant to fetch him his night-gown and calls Varro and Claudius, two of his officers, to sleep in his tent. Lucius sings but soon falls asleep. Throughout this section of the scene Brutus is kindly and tender to the boy. We may think of the irony that Brutus should be affectionate to Lucius and inspire such love in Portia, yet have persuaded himself to murder his friend Caesar in cold blood.

Once again, Brutus is now alone at night and unable to sleep. He sits reading. Then he starts with fear as the Ghost of Caesar appears. Brutus wonders whether he is imagining it, but we see the Ghost and hear it speak. It calls itself Brutus' 'evil spirit' (l. 280). All it has come to announce is that Brutus will see it at Philippi. The phrase 'at Philippi' is heard three times (ll. 281, 283, 284) and then the Ghost vanishes.

Brutus rouses the others in the tent but no one has seen the Ghost apart from himself. He decides to begin the march to Philippi – the setting, as it turns out, for one of the most decisive battles in history.

ACT V SCENE i

The last act takes place at Philippi. In this first scene the two forces meet. Octavius and Antony enter first and Octavius expresses surprise that Brutus and Cassius should openly challenge them rather than keep in the hills and wait. Antony's theory is that it is an attempt to give the impression of a confidence which they do not in fact possess. They quarrel briefly about which flank each should occupy, and Octavius anxiously warns Antony that the time will come when he will 'cross' him (l. 20). (Shakespeare dramatizes this next important phase of Roman history in his later play, *Antony and Cleopatra*.)

The opposing army enters, and the four generals step forward to parley. Antony makes clear in the heated exchange that follows that the issue is still the death of Caesar and that he and Octavius are committed to avenge that death. The taunting between the pairs of generals takes the form of accusations of cowardice and flattery, and silly personal abuse: Brutus calls Octavius 'Young man' (l. 60) and Cassius calls him 'A peevish schoolboy' (l. 61). Cassius calls Antony 'a masquer and a reveller' (l. 62) and Antony responds by calling him 'Old Cassius' (l. 63).

Octavius and Antony withdraw to prepare for battle. Cassius confides to Messala that it is his birthday, but he fears it will be his deathday too. Despite his previous belief in the philosophy of Epicurus, who had no time for omens and portents (and who therefore emphasized man's freedom of action and control over his own destiny), Cassius has been frightened by two eagles which followed from Sardis but have today flown off and been replaced by ravens, crows and kites which circle overhead as if waiting for carrion.

Cassius is still unhappy that Brutus persuaded him against his will that they should take the attack to Octavius and Antony. He asks Brutus whether he is prepared for the consequences of a defeat in the ensuing battle – namely, to be led in triumph through Rome. Brutus says he is prepared to accept his fate stoically, but that the humiliation of becoming Octavius and Antony's showpiece is something he will not accept. Sensing that they may never meet again, they shake hands.

ACT V SCENE ii

If we assume that Octavius did take the right wing, then Brutus faces him on his own left wing. Brutus believes that Octavius' troops are lacking in zest for the fight. He therefore sends Messala with the message to Cassius that their army should attack.

ACT V SCENE iii

We switch to Cassius on the right wing. Brutus seems to have miscalculated and been overwhelmed by Octavius. Cassius' soldiers are enclosed by Antony's force and Cassius is trying to restrain his men's attempts to flee. Cassius sees his own tents burning and retreats to a hill, sending Titinius forward to discover whether some troops in the distance are on his side or the enemy's. Cassius mentions that he has always been short-sighted. It becomes an ironical comment on the lack of foresight exhibited so often by Brutus. But now Cassius becomes the victim of someone else's poor judgement. Pindarus is peering into the distance watching Titinius as he reconnoitres the field of battle on Cassius' behalf. Pindarus believes he can see Titinius taken prisoner by enemy troops. Shamed that his best friend should thus be captured while he himself does nothing to help, Cassius determines to end his life and asks Pindarus to assist him. Pindarus agrees, and Cassius dies.

But it was all a cruel error. Pindarus had misinterpreted what he saw, the troops who surrounded Titinius and cheered were Brutus' soldiers, and they were cheering because Brutus had won a great victory. Titinius kills himself, overwhelmed by the loss of his friend. When Brutus arrives he grimly comments that Caesar is now having his revenge.

ACT V SCENE iv

A scene of battle. Young Cato is slain. He is Portia's brother, and therefore Brutus' brother-in-law, like Cassius. Gradually Brutus' family is being destroyed. But Young Cato loudly proclaims before he dies that he is the son of the famous Cato. We are reminded of the man who not only fought against Caesar in the civil wars but who lived and died by the ideals of Stoicism – fortitude in the face of suffering and reversal, and suicide in the face of humiliation by his enemies. The allusion to Cato is ominous but it also suggests the code of honour by which we expect Brutus to confront his fate.

One of Brutus' officers, Lucilius, is pretending to be Brutus in order to protect him and mislead the enemy. Antony takes Lucilius prisoner but is not fooled and is clearly now winning the battle.

ACT V SCENE v

Brutus and a handful of his soldiers are exhausted and resting on a rock. Brutus believes he is doomed. Caesar's Ghost fulfilled its prophecy and reappeared last night. He seeks someone to help him end his life, but Clitus and Dardanius and Volumnius all refuse him. Does a loyal friend help his friend to commit suicide? What *is* loyalty? Questions of loyalty and friendship have dogged Brutus. He was Caesar's friend, yet he killed Caesar out of loyalty to his own family's reputation as loyal friends of Rome.

Brutus does not want to be defeated in the battle, he prefers to elude his enemies through suicide, and, only a moment before Antony and Octavius march in, Strato holds the sword and Brutus impales himself upon it.

Octavius is magnanimous in victory, but outdone by Antony who speaks only in praise of Brutus – 'the noblest Roman of them all', a man motivated by 'a general honest thought/And common good to all', a 'gentle' life yet so complete that Nature might boast '"This was a man!"' (ll. 68–75). It is left unclear how sincere such a speaker can be, but he and Octavius seem to be convinced that it has been a glorious and happy day (l. 81).

Characters

JULIUS CAESAR

Shakespeare's Julius Caesar is an ambiguous figure. There is much disagreement among the other characters of the play as to Caesar's true nature, and the play as a whole refuses to commit itself to a single opinion about him.

Compared with Brutus, Cassius and Antony, Caesar's part is a small one, and he is only alive for the first half of the play. Yet his spirit lives on and, as an idea in the minds of men like Antony and Brutus, his influence is felt throughout the remaining action. Antony conceives of his political and military campaign as being, at least in part, an attempt to avenge the death of Caesar. Cassius dies with the words, 'Caesar, thou art revenged,/ Even with the sword that killed thee' (V, iii, 45–6). Brutus comments, 'O Julius Caesar, thou art mighty yet!/Thy spirit walks abroad, and turns our swords/In our own proper entrails' (V, iii, 94–6). Indeed, Brutus has good reason to say this of Caesar's spirit, for the Ghost of Caesar haunts him, appearing both at Sardis and at Philippi (V, v, 18–19). Like Cassius, Brutus dies on his own sword, and his last words are 'Caesar, now be still;/I killed not thee with half so good a will' (V, v, 50–51).

The Caesar that everyone remembers after his death is *not* an ambiguous figure. In so far as anyone comments on his nature, it is to represent him as a great man. For Antony he is 'sweet Caesar' (III, ii, 226), 'mighty Caesar!' and 'the noblest man/That ever livèd' (III, i, 148; 256–7). Brutus talks of his valour, his glory (III, ii, 28; 38) and his greatness (IV, iii, 19).

But while he lives Caesar is by no means this simple paragon. He is treated with immense respect by all who meet him in public, but that is itself an ambiguous fact. Is the respect genuine, or is it induced by fear? Caesar certainly has the power to eliminate anyone who is foolish enough to cross him, as Flavius and Marullus learn to their cost (I, ii, 282–3). Casca may loathe him but when Caesar wishes to speak at the beginning of Act I Scene ii Casca dutifully calls for silence.

Caesar has the power to command love as well as fear. Caesar loves Brutus and Brutus loves him. Caesar names his nephew Octavius as his heir, in place of the son Calphurnia fails to bear him, and Octavius fights loyally to avenge 'Caesar's three and thirty wounds' (V, i, 53). Calphurnia loves her husband and pleads with him not to expose himself to danger by attending the Senate on the Ides of March. Artemidorus warns him not to go. And Antony is someone who not only commits himself to avenge Caesar's death but enjoys the warmth of Caesar's friendship while the Dictator is alive.

Co-existing with the universal show of respect are pockets of hidden resentment and criticism. Flavius and Marullus pay with their lives for speaking out too openly, but Cassius and Casca tell Brutus in confidence of their contempt for Caesar, and they know of others – Metellus Cimber, Decius Brutus, Trebonius and Caius Ligarius – who are already plotting the Dictator's downfall. Then even Brutus, whom Antony describes as 'Caesar's angel' (III, ii, 182), is persuaded to join their conspiracy.

Opposition to Caesar is of two kinds. There are those who hate him personally. Cassius seems to be motivated by envy, by anger that Caesar should have gained a position in Rome which he does not deserve and which unjustly casts Cassius into the shadows. Cassius not only envies Caesar his political position, he holds Caesar in contempt. He regards Caesar as an embarrassment because of certain physical frailties (I, ii, 100–131). We can see for ourselves that Caesar is hard of hearing and is susceptible to irritation and anger, and Casca gives a vivid description of one of Caesar's epileptic fits. Cassius sets great store on the Roman ideal of manliness, and by this standard Caesar is only second-rate.

Brutus, however, joins Cassius' conspiracy not out of envy or contempt for Caesar but because of a principle. The principle is that the Republic must be preserved at all costs. Caesar, in Brutus' opinion, is a threat to the preservation of the Republic and must therefore be removed.

Certainly Caesar has acquired a degree of power almost unprecedented in the history of the Republic. He has been awarded the Dictatorship for life. The ordinary people of Rome are eager to celebrate with him his military triumph over the sons of his old enemy, Pompey (I, i). It seems quite possible that Mark Antony's plan to have Caesar crowned as King of Rome will succeed within weeks, if not days. If this happens, Caesar will wield absolute power, the sort of power which Rome, being a Republic, was normally reluctant to give its rulers (since it would mean the effective destruction of the Republic). It is as if Caesar aspires to a power which belongs to a god rather than to a man.

Shakespeare portrays Caesar as a man much impressed by his own greatness. When he speaks in public he sometimes employs the royal 'we'. At other times he speaks as if he were a third person: 'Caesar is turned to hear' (I, ii, 17), 'Shall Caesar send a lie?' (II, ii, 65). Pride in his own achievements passes beyond dignity into arrogance and vanity. In his imagination his will is as final and constant as the pole star or Mount Olympus, the home of the gods.

But Caesar is no god. His physical frailties reveal him as mortal, and in Act III Scene i we see him die an utterly undignified death. Before that, however, we are given evidence that severely undermines Caesar's own conception of himself.

It is not that he has none of the attributes he claims for himself. Nothing in the play takes away from him the glorious career of the historical Caesar. The public figure of history has to be regarded as part of the Caesar that Shakespeare has created. When Antony refers to his 'conquests, glories, triumphs, spoils' (III, i, 149) we are given no indication that anyone in the play would deny Caesar his record as a political and military figure.

As for the leader we see in action, the impression created by his first entry (I, ii, 1ff.) is of a man firmly in command of his people. We have evidence from the first two scenes that he is popular and knows how to delight the crowd when he appears before them. Brutus can find no fault in Caesar's character as a ruler (II, i, 19–21) and Caesar has retained enough of his political instincts to know that Cassius is not to be trusted, however much Antony may disagree.

But Caesar proceeds to ignore his own insight into Cassius' nature. He proudly proclaims, 'I fear him not' (I, ii, 197). When, the following day, Brutus joins in the assassination and stabs his friend and leader, Caesar's words '*Et tu, Brute?*' reflect not only Brutus' treachery but also Caesar's weakness as a judge of people.

He is equally weak as a judge of his own nature. He prides himself on being constant and immovable, and he is wise enough to know that flattery is a danger to any ruler. Indeed, he claims to be immune to the pressure of those who flatter him for political ends. But then Decius Brutus boasts 'I can o'ersway him; for.../... when I tell him he hates flatterers,/ He says he does, being then most flatterèd' (II, i, 203–8). Decius is absolutely right. Caesar decides not to go to the Capitol on the Ides of March, and is then flattered by Decius into changing his mind.

Caesar is equally inconsistent in his attitude to superstition. He asks Antony to touch Calphurnia to cure her barrenness, and he orders his priests to read the entrails on the Ides of March. Cassius remarks that Caesar is 'superstitious grown of late' (II, i, 195). But Caesar ignores the advice of the Soothsayer and rejects the findings of his priests when they examine the sacrifice he has ordered.

There are clearly contradictions in Caesar's nature, just as there are in others of the major characters in the play. What we can say with certainty is that he is a man whose vanity and misjudgements work to undermine his genuine strengths. We have to conclude that Caesar's virtues made more sense in the past than during the period of the play. All his conquests, glories, triumphs, spoils lie in the past. Pride in achievement has given way to arrogance, vanity and self-deception. He has lost his touch. But, once he is dead, the spirit of the great Caesar is reborn and seems to influence, if not dictate, events.

BRUTUS

Brutus is the most prominent figure in the play, a man whom we get to know well and upon whose decisions the action of the play turns.

But while Shakespeare makes him prominent for us, Brutus himself deliberately shuns public prominence in the first two acts.

Of course, he is a Senator and therefore a public figure from the beginning. But he is withdrawn and reticent in the second scene where Caesar is seen celebrating his military victory over Pompey's sons. Brutus wishes to dissociate himself from the triumphal procession, and when questioned by Cassius he attempts to evade any explanation of his behaviour.

We are naturally curious to know what is going on inside Brutus' mind, and Shakespeare allows us to enter into his thoughts and feelings to a degree that makes him quite unlike any other character in the play. What we discover is that Brutus is, as he himself puts it, 'with himself at war' (I, ii, 46), struggling to reconcile his loyalty to Caesar (who is not only his leader but his friend) and his loyalty to the Republic (which he feels is threatened by Caesar's thirst for personal power).

Brutus is involved in some kind of struggle at every stage of the play, first within his own mind, then in the political and military arena. The initial struggle arises from what he experiences as the tension between private life and public life. He hopes to avoid a public role (either supporting Caesar or else opposing him) by withdrawing into the life of a private citizen. But he cannot do this. As a Senator, as Caesar's friend, and as Cassius' friend, he is forced to respond to events in the public sphere. Furthermore, his attempt to be private leads to mental conflict and anxiety, and he cannot hide this fact from those who know him as a private citizen, Cassius (who is his brother-in-law) and Portia (who is his wife).

Both Cassius and Portia comment upon Brutus' withdrawal. In Act I Scene ii, from line 32 to the end, Cassius analyses Brutus' state of mind, and at II, i, 237–302 Portia tries to make Brutus explain his coldness to her and his neurotic behaviour. Indeed, a considerable amount of what we know about Brutus' character comes from the comments of other characters upon him. But we also learn about him from what he has to say in self-description. In Act I Scene ii, for example, he not only tells Cassius how he is trying to hide the inner conflict he feels about Caesar but asserts one of the principles by which he tries to live his life: 'I love/The name of honour more than I fear death' (ll. 88–9).

In later scenes Brutus is quick to explain his moral opinions and the standards he expects others to live up to. He is proud to be a Roman and believes that he and any other honourable citizen must put the good of Rome before all else. He believes in openness and honesty and trust. Thus, when Cassius suggests that all the conspirators swear an oath of commitment to their cause (II, i, 113), Brutus rejects the idea as offensive:

> *What other bond*
> *Than secret Romans that have spoke the word,*
> *And will not palter?*   (ll. 124–6)

A Roman's word is his bond. It is a cruel irony that Brutus finds it impossible to live up to his ideals: he is forced to deceive and treacherously murder his friend, Caesar, and he leads Rome into anarchy and the hands of those who will destroy the Republican ideals he cherishes.

How does it come about that the idealist becomes a murderer and is finally forced to take his own life? The answer lies to a certain extent in the nature of Brutus' mind and the nature of the ideals which that mind holds to so firmly.

Brutus is a thinker. We observe him wrestling with an intellectual problem in his soliloquy when alone in his orchard (II, i, 10–34). His mind is serious, working slowly and thoroughly over problems, and attempting to find general principles upon which to base his arguments and any decisions he must make. Thus he kills Caesar because he believes that absolute power corrupts absolutely and that kings must have no place in a Roman constitution (II, i, 21–7; 52–4). He ignores Caesar as an individual in this argument, dismissing from his mind his knowledge that Caesar has never acted irrationally or tyrannically (II, i, 19–21). Instead, he concentrates exclusively on theoretical issues: under a Monarchy Caesar could prove to be a tyrant, under a Republic he could not. For Brutus, the logic of this argument is enough to persuade him to kill his friend.

He is drawn to concepts such as liberty and honour and Rome. He kills Caesar in the name of liberty, out of a sense of honour, and in the interests of Rome. Even Antony concedes Brutus' purity of motive and commitment to abstract principles:

> *All the conspirators save only he*
> *Did that they did in envy of great Caesar;*
> *He only, in a general honest thought*
> *And common good to all, made one of them.*

(V, v, 69–72)

Yet Antony can only believe that Brutus was a 'butcher' when he assassinated Caesar (III, i, 255). It is typical of Brutus' mind that he is capable of seeing the assassination in quite another light – a *theoretical* light. In Brutus' imagination, the stabbing of Caesar is a ritual sacrifice on behalf of the Republic. Those who shed his blood are 'sacrificers, but not butchers'. They are 'purgers, not murderers' (II, i, 166; 180).

Of course, a politician needs to be able to inspire the public with his own vision of reality. And, once he has agreed to join them, Brutus succeeds in convincing his fellow conspirators of his ideas. They seem to accept him automatically as their leader, and whenever there is a difference of opinion over tactics or principles Brutus wins the day. In the same way, in his brilliant speech in the Forum, Brutus wins over the hearts and minds of the crowd.

But having won the support of the people, Brutus appears to have no personal ambition to further his own political career. That was never a motive for killing Caesar and now he seems merely intent upon justifying his actions to the crowd. When his audience are actually calling for Brutus to be the next Caesar (III, ii, 51) and offering a crown to this man who will have no kings in Rome (l. 52), he simply honours his promise to Antony and makes way for him to give a speech over Caesar's corpse. In that moment he forfeits all political power in Rome.

Indeed, Brutus' political decisions display consistently bad judgement: he convinces the conspirators that Antony is merely an appendage of Caesar and not to be feared; he trusts Antony's show of friendship after the assassination (III, i, 143ff.); and he yields the stage to Antony in the Forum (III, ii, 62), thereby precipitating the civil war which destroys his own political cause. Even in oratory Antony is his master. All in all, Brutus proves to be easily manipulated, first by Cassius and then by Antony, and makes a series of naive and inept political decisions.

Similarly, on the battlefield Brutus shows some ability (at V, iii, 32, when Cassius believes him to be losing, Brutus is in fact winning the first battle at Philippi), but he displays inexperience and weak strategy when he decides to come down out of the hills and challenge Octavius and Antony in the open plains.

When he finds himself defeated in battle, Brutus decides to take his own life. This is not the act of a man in despair but the expression of another of the ideals which Brutus tries to uphold. When he cannot sleep on the eve of the battle Brutus takes up the book he has been reading (IV, iii, 271–2). Shakespeare seems to regard him as a studious man as well as a deep thinker, and Cassius speaks of his 'philosophy' (IV, iii, 143). This philosophy would seem to be the system of beliefs known as Stoicism – a disregard for personal pain and a belief that the individual must take full responsibility for all his own actions, even to the extent of determining his own death.

Here, once again, Brutus finds that his ideals involve him in a struggle. Having forced himself to kill Caesar, and having experienced the ignominy of being driven out of his beloved Rome, he hears the news that Portia has committed suicide. Brutus bends under the pressure of his grief, and an unattractive element in his nature is revealed. There had always been something priggish about his high-mindedness and his refusal to listen to advice when principles were at stake. Now the burden of his moral, political and military isolation produces cracks in his friendship with Cassius. He accuses Cassius of dishonesty and petulantly displays an unduly high opinion of his own virtue:

> *There is no terror, Cassius, in your threats;*
> *For I am armed so strong in honesty*
> *That they pass by me as the idle wind,*
> *Which I respect not.* (IV, iii, 66–9)

Strangely, Brutus seems willing enough to accept tainted money from

Cassius so long as he is not directly responsible for raising it himself. This is Brutus at his worst, and it shows him weakening in the fight against the tragic consequences of his decision to join the conspiracy against Caesar. But after they have quarrelled Brutus and Cassius apologize to each other and Brutus manages to reassert control over his feelings as a Stoic would always hope to do. As Cassius points out to him, a Stoic will not allow 'accidental evils', i.e. misfortune, to disturb the balance of his mind.

Portia is the daughter of Cato, a man famous for his Stoicism in the face of disaster. She is proud of her parentage but dies unstoically, when the balance of her mind *is* disturbed. Her suicide is a reminder that emotion can override reason and lead a man or woman into a dishonourable death. Brutus himself is worried by this idea and says to Cassius that it is 'cowardly and vile,/For fear of what might fall, so to prevent/The time of life' (V, ii, 103–5). Just as there was a conflict of loyalties over the assassination of Caesar, so Brutus has found in Stoicism a contradiction of principles: is it more cowardly to kill oneself or to live as the prisoner of one's enemy? is it more honourable to suffer indignity with patience or to assert an independent spirit by taking one's own life?

Brutus always seeks to be honourable. He wishes to defend his own honour by acting out of principle at all times. But he also wishes to honour his family name: Cato the Stoic was his father-in-law and his uncle; Lucius Junius Brutus, who liberated Rome from the tyranny of kings, was a distant ancestor. This sense of honour is Brutus' strength, in that it drives him into action and dictates his treatment of his friends and enemies. It even dictates the manner of his death. But it is also his weakness. It distorts his judgement and drives him into a tragic action that destroys him and many others. And by destroying himself, he is destroying a man of much nobility and much humanity.

Brutus is ultimately the focus of our attention and the character with whose destiny we are most involved. Although there is something cold and aloof about him at times, he shows how tender and affectionate he can be in the scenes with Portia (II, i) and the servant boy, Lucius (particularly IV, iii, 229–70). Furthermore, Brutus is himself much loved, as well as much respected. Not only his wife, but Cassius and

Caesar love him, and Casca knows that the ordinary people of Rome love him too: 'O, he sits high in all the people's hearts' (I, iii, 157). Even his enemies recognize in him nobility, magnanimity and wholeness. Antony calls him the noblest Roman of them all: 'His life was gentle, and the elements/So mixed in him, that Nature might stand up/And say to all the world, "This was a man!"' (V, v, 73–5). Whether or not Antony means it, this tribute rings true when we read it or hear it in the theatre.

CASSIUS

Cassius is like his brother-in-law, Brutus, in that they are both great readers and thinkers. But they do not think in the same way. Where Brutus deals in grand, abstract ideas, Cassius works closely on practical issues, the way to get things done, the consequences of having got them done.

In his reading, Brutus seems to study the body of ideas known as Stoicism. Cassius, on the other hand, is a follower of the philosophy of Epicurus, at least until Act V Scene ii where he begins to question the Epicurean disbelief in omens. Epicureanism is a sceptical, doubting philosophy, and Cassius is a man who distrusts the appearance of things. For example, he thinks Caesar is a showman, pretending to an outward show of greatness but lacking in inner substance.

In his turn, Caesar thinks Cassius is a mean, cold, unsensual man, a man with a lean and hungry look, a man who loves no plays and hears no music. 'He is a great observer, and he looks/Quite through the deeds of men . . ./Seldom he smiles, and smiles in such a sort/As if he mocked himself, and scorned his spirit/That could be moved to smile at anything' (I, ii, 201–6).

To Caesar's mind, Cassius thinks too much. He means by this that Cassius is thinking thoughts which spell danger to Caesar's political position. The scorn and mockery which Caesar describes derive, he believes, from Cassius being always uneasy in the presence of anyone greater than himself. In other words he is full of envy. This is probably true. Certainly Cassius is embittered that Caesar, whom he regards as his equal (if not his inferior) as a man, 'Is now become a god, and Cassius is/A wretched creature, and must bend his body/If Caesar carelessly but nod on him' (I, ii, 116–18). All this is deeply felt by Cassius, so that he becomes passionate in his denunciation of the 'vile' Caesar.

His emotional outbursts in the first half of the play are carefully geared to his plan to topple Caesar. He works skilfully on Brutus and Casca as he sets about recruiting them for his conspiracy. In the case of Brutus he has to work hard, argue subtly and act deviously in order to suck him into the plot. All his intelligence and powers of observation are brought to bear on Brutus as he applies moral pressure where Brutus is most responsive. All in all, the creation of the conspiracy is a brilliant achievement.

The problem is that Cassius can only control Brutus to the point of persuading him to join the conspiracy. Thereafter Cassius has lost control. Despite his apparent hardness and scepticism he is weak with Brutus once Brutus is committed to the killing. Brutus takes command. Even when Cassius believes Brutus to be misguided in his judgements, Brutus is allowed to implement his own opinion whenever there is a disagreement over policy. Ironically, Cassius is usually right and Brutus is usually wrong. Thus, for example, Cassius wants Antony killed along with Caesar, Brutus overrules him, and Antony lives to triumph over them both.

The truth is that Cassius not only lacks the will to stand up to Brutus when they differ in matters of practical judgement. It also positively pains him to be in any disagreement with Brutus. He takes their friendship immensely seriously. Far from being cold and mean-spirited, the Cassius of the second half of the play is revealed to be a deeply emotional man, loyal, moved and even hurt where he had once seemed callous and calculating. The man who cynically cheated Brutus with bogus letters, egged him on to kill his friend and participated in the bloody murder himself, is quite broken-hearted to find himself quarrelling with Brutus on the battlefield. Protesting that it must mean that Brutus no longer loves him, Cassius exclaims that he is weary of the world, because he is hated by someone he loves. He could, he says, weep his spirit from his eyes.

Then, when the quarrel is made up, Cassius hears from Brutus that Portia is dead. Cassius is profoundly moved: 'O insupportable and touching loss!' (IV, iii, 149). And he continues to brood over the death even when Brutus himself has turned to the discussion of other matters.

The quarrel between them arises out of Brutus' accusation that Cassius has accepted bribes. No doubt he has. The further accusation that he has then refused to lend Brutus money may be taken as confirming Caesar's view that Cassius is the possessor of a lean and hungry look. For this famous remark is surely not the irrational comment it might at first appear to be. No, it has a psychological penetration that does Caesar credit. Cassius is hungry, not so much for power as for love. If he finds giving so difficult it may be because he has such a persistent need to receive, to take, to feed. He is discontented. He is hungry. 'Would he were fatter!' remarks Caesar, knowing that if he were contented he would be no threat.

This psychological interpretation of Cassius is supported by the side of him that is revealed in the quarrel scene. He can't bear Brutus criticizing him. He can't bear the thought that Brutus doesn't love him. Everything for Cassius is terribly *personal*. Brutus kills Caesar because of an abstract idea about Roman liberty. Cassius, one feels, kills Caesar because he hates him. Then he allows his political and military judgement to be swayed by his personal respect for his friend, Brutus. And, finally, when he challenges Octavius and Antony on the battlefield, he ignores the political differences that divide the two armies and descends to mere personal abuse: Octavius is 'A peevish schoolboy', Antony 'a masquer and a reveller' (V, i, 61; 62).

This abuse arises from an idea which Cassius holds passionately, the idea that a man must be a man. To be *manly* means to be strong and virile. The idea is universal in Shakespeare's Rome, and it even seems to affect the women of the play. Portia lives her life as if she, too, has to be manly. Cassius sneers at Caesar for lacking the qualities of a real soldier. He had to be rescued when he got into difficulties swimming across the river Tiber. In Spain he was reduced by fever to the level of 'a sick girl'. And Cassius claims for himself a superiority over Brutus in terms of his experience and wisdom in military affairs.

In other words, Cassius prizes aggressive masculinity, but knows that manliness also involves practicality and intelligence. Finally, however, Cassius prizes honour above all else. So it is that, rather than suffer the humiliation of being led in triumph through the Roman streets as a defeated soldier, Cassius dies on his own sword.

ANTONY

Cassius is perceptive enough to see two important sides to Antony's character. One is love of pleasure. Cassius calls him 'a masquer and a reveller'. The other is an ability to manipulate men and events to his own advantage. Cassius calls him 'A shrewd contriver'.

Antony is a young man in this play, although not as young as Octavius. According to Brutus he is 'given/To sports, to wildness, and much company' (II, i, 188–9). According to Caesar he 'revels long a-nights' (II, ii, 116). He loves plays, and he takes part in the Lupercalian race in I, ii. When Shakespeare went on to write *Antony and Cleopatra* he imagined an older Antony who had reverted to the love of pleasure and whose political and military judgement suffered as a consequence.

In this play, however, it is Antony the shrewd contriver who emerges. He says little in the first two acts. He is merely Caesar's constant companion in the public scenes. As Caesar's favourite he even displays a dangerous lack of intelligence and perception, advising Caesar that he has nothing to fear from Cassius. Brutus dismisses him as 'but a limb of Caesar' (II, i, 165), but once Caesar is dead Antony is revealed to be a man with all the qualities necessary to win public support in Rome and oust and crush Brutus and Cassius.

First of all, having run away at the news of the assassination, Antony has the courage to walk back into the Capitol and face the assassins. When he sees the corpse of Caesar he dares to address it before speaking to the blood-stained men standing over it, even though they have the means to kill him there and then. Later he has the further courage to face the hostile crowd in the Forum after Brutus has won them over to support the killing of Caesar.

Added to this personal courage is his swift and decisive commitment to action. He accepts the role of Caesar's avenger without hesitation. Horrified by the killing of 'the noblest man/That ever livèd' he unleashes civil war in Rome, confident that it is the expression of 'Caesar's spirit' (III, i, 256–7; 270).

Of course, Antony has plenty to gain from avenging Caesar's death, for it entails his own rise to supreme political power. Shakespeare gives us the room to interpret Antony as either a sincere supporter of a great Roman leader, in whose memory he works to ensure the political security of the Roman people, or else as an ambitious individual, cynically exploiting the name of Caesar in the interests of his own career.

This ambiguity permeates the presentation of the whole of Antony's character. He not only seems to love plays as a spectator, he seems drawn to a kind of theatrical performance in his own life as well. Casca describes how Antony made a public display of offering Caesar the crown. When he gives his funeral oration over Caesar's body he behaves as if he were in a theatre, treating the corpse as if it were a stage-property, producing the will as if it were another stage-property, drawing sympathy from his audience by breaking down and weeping. And the greatest of his histrionic skills is his power with language. Cassius observes that Antony's words 'rob the Hybla bees,/And leave them honeyless' (V, i, 34–5). But, however sweet, they always carry a sting. When he meets with the conspirators after the assassination and when he later addresses the crowd in the Forum Antony proves himself to be a brilliant rhetorician – first evading, blocking and defusing all dangers to himself, then flattering, manipulating, persuading and arousing the people to the point that they will do anything, good or bad, that he directs them to.

His gift extends to situations as well as words. He is a great improviser, seeing and seizing the opportunity to play on his listeners' weaknesses and any material that is to hand. In one case, what is to hand is literally a hand, or, rather, a number of hands. When he faces the assassins at Act III Scene i, l. 184 he seizes their bloody hands, as if he were befriending them but, in fact, to seal his own bloody pact with his dead friend. As he shakes each hand in turn he names each assassin. The show of trust and intimacy masks the real effect. Antony is naming each of those he intends to punish. He is exerting and celebrating his power over each silent murderer, as he identifies them by name and holds each hand in his. The blood that thereby accumulates on his hand seems to signify his entering into their circle, but in fact it is Caesar's blood which he is gathering to himself and employing as a signal that he will go on to avenge the act of shedding it. This cunning gesture typifies the control which Antony seems effortlessly to exercise over the conspirators from the moment he hears of Caesar's death.

Caesar and Cassius and Brutus, true to a Roman's education, are all first-rate orators, but Antony is their master. He promises Brutus that he will not denigrate the conspirators in his Forum speech. He sticks to the letter of this promise, but violates its spirit, praising them so relentlessly that a word like 'honourable' is transformed into a term of stinging abuse. How absurd that he should claim to be no orator, 'But, as you know me all, a plain blunt man/ ... /For I have neither wit, nor words, nor worth,/Action, nor utterance, nor the power of speech/To stir men's blood' (III, ii, 219–24). What gall! He subtly takes over the crowd's head of emotion, previously stirred up by Brutus' brilliant speech, to transform a movement to make Brutus the next Caesar into a movement to drive the conspirators out of Rome. And when he has done it, he appears to have no moral attitude to the frightening consequences of his oratory. He is triumphant. He is not himself swept away by his own power, the magical power to transform men's minds and hearts, the actor's power to impose his own design on his audience's imagination. No, he is in control, but quite cynically and deliberately abandons his control over the mob. He knows that any destruction of the city can only make it easier for him to fill the political vacuum created by the flight of Brutus and Cassius: 'Now let it work. Mischief, thou art afoot,/Take thou what course thou wilt' (III, ii, 261–2).

The seemingly frivolous playboy of the first two acts has become a man capable of cold calculation and harsh measures. He and Octavius ruthlessly purge their enemies, commanding the execution of between seventy and a hundred Senators. He names his nephew, Publius, among those who must die, and betrays no remorse. He sneers at Lepidus behind his back ('A barren-spirited fellow') and explains that he is cynically employing him only for as long as he will serve the interests of himself and Octavius. Having used Caesar's will to convince the Plebeians of Caesar's generosity, Antony now sends Lepidus to fetch it so that he can alter its terms in his own interests.

For all that Shakespeare appears to darken Antony's character in the second half of the play, he still allows us to see him in a positive light if we choose to do so. There may be strains showing in the relationship between him and Octavius when the latter's military advice is ignored, but Octavius is the junior soldier and Antony's opinion is vindicated in so far as victory at Philippi is theirs. Antony's victory speech praises Brutus. We recall that, for Antony, Caesar had been the greatest man that ever lived. Yet here he describes Brutus as 'the noblest Roman of them all'. Is this the honey-tongued politician again, mouthing platitudes merely for public consumption? We can never say, but Shakespeare provides no evidence to persuade us that Antony is not moved and magnanimous in his victory.

OCTAVIUS CAESAR

The historical Octavius was Caesar's great-nephew and adopted son. Shakespeare is silent over these facts. He merely mentions that Caesar had summoned Octavius to Rome, just before the assassination.

We first see him in Act IV, when he arrives in Rome and joins with Antony and Lepidus to form the Second Triumvirate. This is the name given to the arrangement by which the three men shared the rule of Rome after Brutus and Cassius had been driven out of the city.

Brutus and Cassius both scorn Octavius for his youth ('a peevish schoolboy'). He is clearly the junior party with Antony, whom he irritates at Philippi by disagreeing over military strategy.

Nevertheless, Octavius is a coming force. In Shakespeare's *Antony and Cleopatra* Octavius goes on to prove a sounder general and more skilful politician than Antony. Here, he is a young man quickly developing into the figure of the later play. Despite some squeamishness about Antony's shabby treatment of Lepidus, Octavius is fully prepared to inform Lepidus that his brother must be put to death in the interests of the Triumvirate's purge of political opponents. He eagerly enters into the exchange of verbal abuse that precedes the battle of Philippi, then cuts short the debate and urges Antony to start fighting. He is even given the play's closing speech, paying a statesman's tribute to the dead enemy, Brutus, before turning enthusiastically to the prospect of dividing 'the glories of this happy day'.

Shakespeare provides no comment on Octavius' opinion that the battle has resulted in a glorious and happy outcome. We have been involved closely with the fortunes of Brutus, and the battle must therefore seem to us to have a tragic dimension to it. But Shakespeare's original audience would have been well aware that Octavius was going to become the Emperor Augustus and preside over the Roman Empire, one of the most important institutions in the history of the Western World. Insofar as the battle of Philippi heralded the Imperial phase of Roman history, the phase which was eventually to include the official adoption of Christianity, many Elizabethans must have felt that Octavius was justified in calling the day of his victory a happy and glorious one.

CASCA

As the novelist E. M. Forster once pointed out, Shakespeare is not consistent in his portrait of Casca:

Casca first appears as extremely polite and indeed servile to Caesar. 'Peace, ho! Caesar speaks,' he cries. Then he shows himself to Brutus and Cassius as a sour blunt contradictious fellow, who snaps them up when they speak and is grumpy when they invite him to supper. You may say this is subtlety on Shakespeare's part, and that he is indicating that Casca is a dark horse. I don't think so. I don't think Shakespeare was bothering about Casca – he is merely concerned to make the action interesting and he alters the character at need.

Forster makes an important point here. The Casca of the early scene is not presented as a *character* and the audience is not interested in him until later in the play. It certainly would not be wrong to think out why Casca should show no public resentment of Caesar in the early scene. After all, Flavius and Marullus, we hear, have been put to death for their opposition to Caesar. But Shakespeare has nobody inform us that he *is* Casca in the early scene and he makes no impact on an audience *as* Casca. No, at this stage, he is merely one of those in the crowd of Senators who accompany Caesar in his procession.

If we can agree, then, that Shakespeare may not always be bothering too much about the consistency and roundedness of his characters we can proceed with Casca. And it is in the scene where he describes how Antony offered the crown to Caesar that Casca makes a vivid impression on an audience. He clearly hates Caesar and is disgusted by what he regards as Caesar's play-acting. He thinks Caesar really wants to be crowned but knows he will gain popularity by publicly refusing it.

This does not mean that Casca pities the people for being abused by their political leaders. On the contrary, Casca despises them for being so gullible. Indeed, his language becomes crude and offensive whenever he describes the working people of Rome – they are 'sweaty' and 'stinking', they are 'the tag-rag people', 'the common herd'.

Brutus is quite surprised by Casca's tone of contempt for almost everyone: 'What a blunt fellow is this grown to be!/He was quick mettle when he went to school' (I, ii, 292–3). In fact, Casca's cynicism stretches to Brutus himself, whose popularity with the people makes Casca bitter (I, iii, 157–60). Antony refers to him as 'the envious Casca' (III, ii, 176).

But Casca has courage. He also has a practical intelligence (he urges Brutus to address the people after the assassination). And he has a defender in Cassius, who attempts to explain away his sour, insensitive attitudes and language as an affectation.

PORTIA

Neither Portia nor Calphurnia makes any significant impact on public events in this play. It is a man's world that Shakespeare portrays. While Brutus and Caesar are both shown as listening to their wives' opinions, they nevertheless go on to act as if they had never been expressed.

But Portia is a perceptive and intelligent woman. To her mind she and Brutus are equals: she is his 'self', his 'half', and marriage 'did incorporate and make us one' (II, i, 273). This confidence in their relationship is challenged by Brutus' behaviour in the early part of the play. They have always been a close, loving couple, but he has recently become moody and withdrawn, preoccupied and anxious. She demands an explanation, and when he attempts to put her off by saying he has been ill she tells him the truth: 'You have some sick offence within your mind' (II, i, 268).

Furthermore, she informs her husband that he must tell her what the thoughts are that are making him behave so strangely. He must tell her 'by the right and virtue of my place' (II, i, 269). This belief in her self and in her role in marriage is much stronger than Calphurnia's, and Brutus' love and respect for her seems much stronger than does Caesar's for his wife. Brutus yields to her pressure and movingly exclaims, 'You are my true and honourable wife,/As dear to me as are the ruddy drops/That visit my sad heart' (II, i, 288–90). Therefore, we assume from what passes later (in Act II Scene iv), he tells her the secrets of his heart. The sick offence is his growing involvement in the conspiracy to kill Caesar.

Once she is told, Portia discovers that another of her firm beliefs is challenged. She considers herself to be the equal, not only of Brutus, but of any man – and, in particular, in terms of courage and self-control. Courage and self-control are fundamental to the philosophy known as Stoicism, and Portia is proud to be the daughter of the famous statesman and Stoic, Marcus Porcius Cato. Cato committed suicide rather than endure the indignity of being captured by his enemies. Portia demonstrates to Brutus that she is her father's daughter by showing him a wound in her thigh, a wound she has inflicted on herself in order to test her ability to endure pain.

This confidence in her own courage and self-control is rocked by the news that Brutus intends to assassinate Caesar. What she discovers is that her constancy (rigid loyalty and self-denial) is tested to breaking point by the weight of the information she has been given: 'I have a man's mind, but a woman's might./How hard it is for women to keep counsel!' (II, iv, 8–9). She fears she may inadvertently betray her husband and, on the morning of the conspiracy, we observe her feverishly pacing about her house and feeling faint.

Finally, we learn that Portia's patience is not only tested but broken. Patience in the Stoic tradition involves the ability to withstand suffering, but Portia is led to kill herself by her impatience: unable to endure the absence of her husband, once he has fled Rome, and afraid of the growing strength of Antony and Octavius, she goes mad and swallows fire. This is not the true Stoic's death but an indignity.

And yet that is not quite the end, for Shakespeare shows us Brutus receiving the news of Portia's death. His reaction is complicated by his own Stoicism, his own struggle not to give in to emotion, but it is clear that both he and Cassius are deeply moved by the tragic news of 'this noble wife' (II, i, 303).

CALPHURNIA

Calphurnia is less of an individual than Portia. She is merely Caesar's wife. Whereas Portia's own conception of honour is as important to her as is her love for Brutus, Calphurnia's actions all arise out of her relationship with her husband. And Caesar is full of his own importance and on the defensive if his wife appears to be affecting his decisions in life.

Thus, in the scene when, early on the morning of the Ides of March, she argues with Caesar that he should not go to the Senate House, he is easily persuaded by Decius Brutus that he will be a laughing-stock if he gives in to his wife's fears. Those fears are based on a nightmare she has had during her sleep. She has dreamed that Caesar's statue is running with blood. She has cried out in her sleep, 'Help, ho! They murder Caesar!' (II, ii, 3). She has heard reports of extraordinary portents observed by Roman citizens in the streets. She senses in all this a warning of her husband's death, and she is, of course, absolutely right to regard her fears as prophetic.

Up to this point in the play she has shown no spirit. She seems to have failed Caesar in not bearing him any children and he publicly describes her as sterile. She takes orders in silence. But when Caesar has an epileptic fit Brutus notices that Calphurnia's cheek is pale: we don't know why, but her pallor suggests the repression of feeling, shock or anger or anxiety which must not be acknowledged or spoken.

And now, when her husband's life seems to be at stake, she finds the courage to stand up to him. When he dismisses her fears she is prepared to criticize him, and even to appear a fool herself in order to protect him:

> *Alas, my lord,*
> *Your wisdom is consumed in confidence.*
> *Do not go forth today: call it my fear*
> *That keeps you in the house, and not your own.*

> (II, ii, 48–51)

She has become his partner – 'We'll send Mark Antony to the Senate House,/And he shall say you are not well today' – and he agrees to her request. But his pride is such that he intends to have his absence explained away as his wife's 'humour', i.e. whim, and when Decius flatters him Caesar quickly changes his mind, calling her foolish. He sets off for the Capitol, and we hear no more of Calphurnia.

THE PEOPLE

The play begins with a scene portraying the common people of Rome. We hear of their trades and their shops, and that one is a carpenter and another a cobbler. But they are on holiday. They appear to have chosen to take a day off work in order to stand in the street, watching and cheering their Dictator as he passes by in triumph.

Caesar may have been fighting a civil war against his fellow Romans, but the crowd seem happy enough to treat him as if he were a national hero. Indeed, they seem to want heroes, just as they are drawn to public spectacles. We hear that it is not long since Pompey was their hero, and that when he passed in procession through these very streets they were packing the windows and roof-tops in order to see him and shout their approval. And later in the play, with Caesar dead, they have switched their hero-worship to someone else, to Brutus:

> Bring him in triumph home unto his house.
> Give him a statue with his ancestors.
> Let him be Caesar.
>   Caesar's better parts
> Shall be crowned in Brutus.
> We'll bring him to his house with shouts and clamours.
>   (III, ii, 49–53)

On the other hand, they will turn on their heroes. Caesar has triumphed over Pompey and they have now forgotten Pompey. When Caesar is dead Brutus quickly convinces them that 'This Caesar was a tyrant' and that they are well rid of him (III, ii, 70–71). Yet, when Antony has finished with them, they have decided that Brutus is a traitor and a villain, that he must be killed and his house burnt to the ground. Caesar has become their hero once again and they will do anything to avenge his death. It is a devastating portrait of fickleness and gullibility. The people seem quite unable to resist the power of the politicians' words. They have no memory, no judgement, and yet a desperate need to side emotionally and often violently with those they consider to be heroes against those they consider to be villains.

The two politicians who confront them in the opening scene are their own elected representatives in the government of Rome. Flavius and Marullus are known as the Tribunes of the People. But they are not men of the people, they are not Plebeians, they are Patricians (i.e. aristocrats, like Brutus and Cassius and Caesar). They display no fellow-feeling for the common people. Indeed, like almost all the Patricians except, possibly, Brutus, they seem to hold the people in contempt. They abuse them to their faces as 'blocks', 'stones', 'worse than senseless things' (I, i, 35). Behind their backs they refer to the Plebeians dismissively as 'the vulgar' (I, i, 70).

For Flavius and Marullus, the common people are tools in a political power-struggle. Although they are like putty in the hands of the politicians, their support is nevertheless a necessity for those who wish to wield power in Rome. The power-struggle is between members of the Patrician class, and between parties made up of those Patricians. Flavius and Marullus are clearly old supporters of Pompey. They detest Caesar and are working to undermine his authority. Their aim in the opening scene is to clear the people off the streets so that Caesar's public procession will look to have been a failure.

To this end the Tribunes tear down the decorations in the streets put up by Caesar's supporters. Caesar's response is to have them killed, as we learn (I, ii, 282). This information reminds us that, for all the apparent spontaneity in the turnout of the people to line Caesar's route through the city, triumphal processions are carefully organized political events, and that even at this point the people are being manipulated by those who wish to rule Rome.

Caesar is always conscious of his public image. Decius knows this when he works on Caesar to persuade him to attend the Senate even though Caesar has decided he will not go (II, ii). Decius plays on the fact that Caesar does not want to suffer the public indignity of appearing to be under the thumb of Calphurnia. This is a minor weakness (although, of course, one that proves to be fatal). But his ability to project his image to his political advantage is a major strength. And Casca tells us how skilfully Caesar works on the emotional sympathies of the crowd when he describes the off-stage scene in which Antony offers Caesar the crown and Caesar refuses it. Three times it is offered, and three times we hear the roar of the crowd as Caesar says no. We can only assume it is a roar of approval.

Once Caesar has been killed, Brutus feels he must speak to the people. This is partly because he wishes to make public the fact, and the significance (as he sees it), of the killing:

> ... *let us bathe our hands in Caesar's blood*
> *Up to the elbows, and besmear our swords;*

> *Then walk we forth, even to the market-place,*
> *And waving our red weapons o'er our heads,*
> *Let's all cry, 'Peace, freedom, and liberty!'*

(III, i, 106- 10)

Partly, Brutus wants to calm the people, for their own good and for the good of the city. Trebonius describes how, after the immediate shock of the assassination, 'Men, wives, and children stare, cry out, and run,/As it were doomsday' (III, i, 97–8). But when Antony says that he wishes to address the people at Caesar's funeral, Brutus realizes that he must retain the political initiative by speaking to them first.

In the Forum there are individual voices to be heard calling out from the crowd gathered to hear the funeral speeches, but Shakespeare merely distinguishes them by numbers (First Plebeian, Second Plebeian, etc.). They pride themselves on being men of judgement, demanding satisfaction as to why their leader has been murdered, and proposing to compare the reasons Brutus gives in the Forum with those Cassius is giving in the adjoining street. On the whole, however, they take their cues from those who address them, displaying slow reasoning powers but alarming speed in changing opinion and surrendering to emotion. By the end of the scene they have been made fools of by Antony. They are all for rushing off to Brutus' house to kill him, but Antony reminds them that they have forgotten to hear the contents of Caesar's will, and their greed makes them hang on, falling more deeply under his spell. He proceeds to work them up until they are overtaken by a kind of hysteria, prepared to vandalize property and take human life in their lust to avenge their beloved Caesar's death. Antony is entirely cynical in his treatment of them. They are his weapon against Brutus and Cassius. He displays the same contempt towards them that the Tribunes had shown in I, i.

Casca is the most extreme of their critics. For him they are 'the rabblement', 'the tag-rag people', 'the common herd' (I, ii, 242; 256; 262), their hands are chapped, their night-caps sweaty and their breath offensive. This language and this attitude tells us as much about Casca as it does about the common people, but after Antony's speech in the Forum the mob live up to the contempt in which the Patricians hold them throughout the play. When we witness the mindless brutality of the scene in which they lynch Cinna the poet (III, ii) we despise them. It is a terrifying incident. The mob is not only shown up for their ignorance, confusing one Cinna for another, but go on to beat up the poet even once his true identity is known. It amuses them to kill him and, no doubt, they hate him for his learning because it is a sign of privilege.

This last thought might remind us, nevertheless, that this is the first time that the people have proved themselves anything but docile members of an abused class. If we think back to the beginning of the play the Plebeians were never shown to be a discontented group. They were not hungry, or out of work, or resentful of their leaders. The Cobbler and the Carpenter were genial and even witty, the crowd as a whole were easily cowed and slunk home guiltily under the Tribunes' attack. Even during the Forum scene, their violent passions are aroused in defence of one or other of their leaders from the Patrician class, rather than out of personal grievances or in order to advance their own interests. However much contempt we may sometimes feel for the Plebeians we must remember the contempt Shakespeare sometimes makes us feel for the Patricians, and particularly in those scenes where the Patricians take advantage of the worst aspects of the Plebeians' natures.

Commentary

THE HISTORICAL SETTING

Julius Caesar is not a textbook of Ancient History. Shakespeare deliberately distorts history in order to make his play work. Thus, he gives the impression that Caesar was murdered within a day or two of his triumphal entry into Rome, whereas in fact there was a gap of some four months between the two events. The effect is to make Caesar's death more than just a death, more even than a particularly bloody assassination. His moment of glory is so short-lived and so closely associated with his death that we are invited to interpret the relationship between the two events. What is Shakespeare saying by linking them? Are we meant to be appalled that a great man's life should be so suddenly and tragically cut short when he is at the height of his power? Or do we take his death to be a just comment on the vanity of a weak man carried away by a search for power and public acclaim?

Shakespeare was not a scrupulous historian. Quite apart from his willingness to alter historical facts, he relied heavily on one history book, a recent translation of a readable but unreliable work by Plutarch (a Greek historian born in the first century A.D.). But Shakespeare would also have had a general knowledge of Roman history which many of us do not have.

This is because any educated Elizabethan (even if, like Shakespeare, he had only been to school and not gone on to University) would have studied Latin and learnt a great deal of classical mythology and the history of Rome. Indeed, we can assume that the original audience of *Julius Caesar* knew not only the outline of Caesar's career but had some sense of his significance in the history of Europe. However, the

Elizabethans seem to have been strongly divided over what that significance was.

There were two conflicting opinions of Julius Caesar, and as a result there were two opinions of Brutus. Some regarded Caesar as a hero, and Brutus as a murderous villain. Some took quite the opposite view, seeing Caesar as a tyrant and Brutus as a noble liberator. In order to understand why there should have been this kind of disagreement, it is necessary to know a little of the history of Rome.

Put in very simple terms, the history of Rome can be divided into three phases. At first (from about 753 B.C. onwards) Rome had been ruled by kings. They were elected for life and had absolute power. Then, in 510 B.C., the tyrannical Tarquinius the Proud was driven out of Rome by Lucius Junius Brutus (whom the Brutus of this play claims as an ancestor). This revolt ended the first phase, the phase which Brutus and Cassius would look back on as the phase of the Tyrants.

The second phase is known as the Republic. This lasted almost five hundred years, ending with the death of Caesar in 44 B.C. Although the constitution changed a certain amount during this long period, it was always built on a system of government involving a Senate and two officers, who came to be known as Consuls. The Consuls were elected for one year only, and it was hoped that each would act as a check on the other. In times of extreme crisis a Dictator, who wielded absolute power, would be appointed. But a Dictator would have to step down after six months, at which point the normal constitution would be revived.

There is clearly a democratic element in this arrangement. The Consuls were elected and were answerable to the Senate. The ordinary working people, the Plebeians, elected two representatives to participate in the government of Rome. In this play Shakespeare introduces us to these Tribunes of the People, Flavius and Marullus, in Act I Scene i.

On the other hand, the Tribunes were drawn from the ranks of the aristocracy, and certain aristocratic families dominated the Senate and therefore the choice of Consuls. The Roman Republic was a mixed constitution, a blend of democracy and aristocracy. The one thing it was not, however, was a monarchy. The Kings, the Tyrants, had been driven out, and kept out for five centuries.

But the Republic began to break down. In 82 B.C. Sulla was made

Dictator for life. After his abdication a mere three years later there was a struggle for power between two parties. The more conservative Optimates came to be associated with Pompey, while the rather more democratic Populares came to be associated with Julius Caesar. A personal power struggle emerged between these two men.

In 60 B.C. Crassus joined Pompey and Caesar in a private pact to share power in Rome. This pact of three leaders was known as the First Triumvirate. It soon collapsed, but it revealed how ambitious individuals could override the constitution and make their own arrangements for the rule of Rome.

In 49 B.C., after two years in which Pompey ruled as sole Consul in Rome, civil war broke out between Pompey and Caesar. The following year, Pompey was defeated in battle and Caesar became Dictator. Pompey's supporters continued to resist until October 45 B.C. when, having finally overcome Pompey's sons in Spain, Caesar entered Rome in triumph.

This is the point at which Shakespeare's play begins. It is peopled with famous historical figures – not only Julius Caesar and Octavius Caesar, Mark Antony, Brutus and Cassius, but also Cicero, the greatest of all the Roman orators. We hear references to other famous figures of the recent past, such as Lucius Junius Brutus, Pompey the Great and Cato, who was Brutus' father-in-law. Cato had died fighting against Caesar in 46 B.C. Brutus and Cassius had also been supporters of Pompey at the start of the civil war, but had been won over, like Cicero, to Caesar's side.

Shakespeare does not call attention to this last fact, but it is interesting to notice how all the opposition to Caesar in the play is drawn from the ranks of those who had once supported Pompey. Perhaps it is no accident that Cassius arranges to meet some of his fellow conspirators at Pompey's Porch (I, iii, 126). It is certainly a deliberate irony that Caesar should die at the base of Pompey's statue, as if Pompey were wreaking his revenge over his old adversary (III, i, 115)

In 46 B.C. Caesar had had himself declared Dictator for ten years. The following year this was converted into Dictatorship for life, and the year after that he was offered the crown, but refused. He was clearly king in all but name. In Shakespeare's play Brutus and the other conspirators clearly fear that it will only be a matter of time before Caesar accepts the crown, and then the Republic will be finished.

It is in the light of these facts that some Elizabethans regarded Caesar as the villain and Brutus as the hero. Caesar was in danger of becoming a despot and destroying the Republic, which, for some of Shakespeare's contemporaries, represented the greatest period of Roman history. In this interpretation, Caesar's murderers were heroic liberators, fighting for the Republic and removing a tyrant in the same way that Lucius Junius Brutus had removed the despotic Tarquinius five centuries before.

In order to understand the contrary view, that Caesar was a hero and Brutus a villain, it is necessary to recognize that Brutus had murdered one of the most famous and influential men in history. Caesar was a great soldier, statesman and writer. But having said this it is also necessary to examine something of the subsequent history of Rome, especially as it concerns Octavius Caesar, the young man whom Caesar had adopted as his heir, and who enters Shakespeare's play in the second half.

The result of the assassination of Caesar was not the immediate revival of the Republic, as Brutus might have hoped. Instead there was another period of civil war and then the eventual victory of the Second Triumvirate (Mark Antony, Octavius Caesar and Lepidus) at the battle of Philippi in 42 B.C. (In fact there were two battles, but Shakespeare collapses them into one to simplify the ending of the play.) Eleven years later, at the battle of Actium, Octavius emerged as sole ruler of the Roman world. He called himself the Emperor Augustus.

This marks the beginning of the third phase, the period known as the Empire. It was in this phase that Rome adopted Christianity when the Emperor Constantine was converted and, in A.D. 330, moved the capital of the Empire from Rome to Byzantium. For those Elizabethans who emphasized the role of the Roman Empire in establishing Christianity as a world religion, Julius Caesar and Octavius Caesar stood out as architects of that Empire, and therefore as making possible the eventual growth of the Church. For them, Brutus was a wrecker, holding back the evolution of the Empire out of the Republic.

As for Shakespeare himself, his play provides material for both parties in the controversy to draw on. Like Plutarch, whose *Lives of the Noble Grecians and Romans* he had clearly studied, Shakespeare seems to have been able to see the good and bad on both sides. His Caesar certainly has faults, but then so has his Brutus. Yet they are both honoured in death, even by those who were their enemies when they were alive.

POLITICS

Julius Caesar is about the assassination of one of the world's most famous leaders. It examines the way in which the assassination comes about. It presents the assassination in all its bloody brutality. And then it examines the aftermath, the consequences of the coup. It is a fascinating analysis of the nature of politics.

The political background to the play is the struggle of Caesar against Pompey the Great. This struggle continues throughout the play, even though Pompey is dead before it begins and Caesar is dead by the end of Act III Scene i. At the end of the play, Caesar's heir Octavius is celebrating victory over Brutus and Cassius, who had originally been Pompey's supporters. But by this stage it has become clear that Octavius is involved in a further struggle, the struggle for power between himself and the other members of the Triumvirate, Antony and Lepidus.

The play demonstrates two fundamental facts. First of all, nothing stands still in politics. The beginning of the play is not the beginning of the political story, and the end of the play is not the end of that story. Politics is a continuing story, a process in which power moves from faction to faction, and the factions themselves dissolve as new factions arise.

The other fact is that politics is about power. For the unscrupulous, power is the end of all political activity. For them and for everyone else, including the most scrupulous and benevolent, power is the necessary means for achieving any ends at all.

We live in a monarchy, but our kings and queens have very little power. Shakespeare also lived in a monarchy, but in his day a king or queen wielded immense power. The Rome of Shakespeare's play is not a monarchy. but a republic – a political system which had deliberately turned its back on kings. Brutus believes that Rome must never have another king. But Caesar is being encouraged by Antony (I, ii) to seal his victory in the civil wars by assuming absolute power and accepting the title of King.

Brutus and Cassius join with others to kill Caesar. But their motives for so doing are very different. Cassius seems to be driven by intense hatred for the man. He envies Caesar his position and his removal from that position would give Cassius great personal satisfaction. But Brutus loves Caesar. His loyalties are thus divided between personal friendship and the belief that Caesar is a potential tyrant. Once Caesar agrees to be king he will be legally invested with absolute power and he will then no longer be answerable to the Roman Senate and people. Brutus' belief is a product of his political idealism. The *possibility* that Caesar might become a despot is sufficient to persuade Brutus that he is duty bound to make such an eventuality impossible. And this means he must destroy Caesar.

The play demonstrates the fatal process of reasoning that drives a sincere, well-meaning man to murder in the name of a political ideal. And it also demonstrates that in politics, idealists are obliged to rub shoulders, and even enter into solemn pacts, with people motivated by personal ambition, envy, greed, irrational hatred.

Political action always involves political alliances between individuals who calculate that they cannot achieve power on their own. But within each faction there must be mutual trust. Brutus and Cassius disagree about whether or not Antony should be killed at the same time as Caesar. In order to keep the alliance together Cassius is prepared to allow Brutus' view to prevail. After the assassination, however, more differences open up, and lack of military cohesion ultimately brings defeat and death to Brutus and Cassius at the battle of Philippi. But there is division in their opponents' camp too. Although the Triumvirate of Antony, Octavius and Lepidus holds together for the duration of the play it is clear that the day is not far off when the individual ambitions of the triumvirs will put too great a strain on their alliance.

The original conspiracy comes into being through Cassius' skill in co-ordinating the different forms of opposition to Caesar's political rule, so that they can be forged into a single faction committed to a single end, the death of Caesar. Shakespeare shows us a political regime which brutally resists opposition, and therefore a regime which can only be overthrown by violent means. It is a society in which people keep quiet about their political opinions if they are critical of Caesar. Flavius and Marullus don't keep quiet (I, i) and pay for their folly with their lives (I, ii). Casca is secretly contemptuous of Caesar but is publicly an obsequious yes-man (I, ii). Brutus tries to pretend he is nothing to do with Caesar's triumph and is loath to say anything at all about his political opinions (I, ii).

When the violence erupts it is spectacular. Caesar is stabbed many times over, each conspirator in turn making a political gesture by shedding the enemy's blood and shedding it in public. But Caesar's death leaves an immediate power vacuum. He is not king, so he has no heir to his power. It is there for anyone to seize. Brutus seizes it. He goes quickly to the public Forum to address the people of Rome, intending to publicize and justify the coup. And this nearly works. Not only is he seemingly vindicated as an individual, not only does the public seem to accept his notion that the killing was not murder but a political necessity, but he seems to have gained sufficient popularity to fill the power vacuum and rule as Caesar himself.

By securing the support of the people Brutus seems to have acted like a skilled politician. Under the Roman constitution which Brutus wishes to preserve, the ordinary people have a limited voice through their elected Tribunes. But under any system the people are an essential element in the political equation. Political leaders are powerless unless they can control the populace and their active support is preferable to their enforced submission. All the major politicians in *Julius Caesar* endeavour to woo the people, and all succeed at some point in the play. At different times and in quick succession Pompey (before the play begins), Caesar (I, ii), Brutus (III, ii) and then Antony (also III, ii), are the darlings of the crowd. We hear about and directly observe a series of occasions on which the mob is won over by the oratory and theatricality of the politicians (I, ii, and III, ii). The common people seem fickle, greedy, easily flattered and violent; the politicians seem cynical and insincere, opportunists and showmen.

The aftermath of the assassination is a devastating portrait of political struggle, in which the cleverer politicians easily outwit the more inept. The main weakness of those who led the coup turns out to be that they lack any plan once Caesar is dead. They have no idea what they are going to do with the power they have won. And they have no idea how they are going to hold on to that power.

Cassius sets up the conspiracy. He seems to understand the psychology of individual Senators, and he senses that Antony represents a threat to the coup. But he allows Brutus to lead the alliance. Brutus' idealism blinds him to political realities, the chief of which is that Antony is not to be trusted. Brutus entrusts Antony with the two elements he needs to win power, Caesar's corpse and a public platform in the Forum. Brutus thereby loses the initiative to Antony, Antony uses the corpse as a means to win the support of the people, and unleashes anarchy in the streets. Public disorder can only destabilize the ruling faction, so Brutus is driven out of the city, leaving a second political vacuum. Antony and Octavius eagerly step in to fill it.

Once in charge the leaders of the counter-coup ruthlessly eliminate all political opposition within Rome and follow this up by hunting down and defeating Brutus and Cassius on the battlefield. Antony may have no more idea of what he intends to do with power than Brutus had. Perhaps he has less, for Brutus would seem at least to have wished to preserve the constitution. But Antony knows that having acquired power he must keep it, and that, in order to do that, he must exercise it, ruthlessly.

THE ART OF PERSUASION

Because it is primarily a play about political activity, much of *Julius Caesar* is taken up with scenes in which characters are shown in debate and attempting to persuade other characters to change their views.

In the opening scene the Tribunes are persuading a crowd of

Plebeians to leave the streets and go back to work. In the next scene Cassius attempts to persuade Brutus to join his conspiracy against Caesar. As the play unfolds, we encounter any number of characters arguing, coaxing, pleading, challenging: Brutus argues himself into killing Caesar; Portia argues him into telling her his plan; the Soothsayer, Artemidorus and Calphurnia all urge Caesar not to go to the Capitol; Decius urges him to go; the conspirators plead with Caesar for Publius Cimber's life, and Cinna the poet pleads with the mob for his own life; Cassius and Brutus quarrel and another poet begs them to make peace.

A Roman education devoted much time to the study of what was called Rhetoric. Rhetoric was the art of persuasion and, in particular, the art of public speaking. In the law courts and in political debate, men like Cicero helped to establish a method of constructing and ornamenting arguments that became famous in the Roman world and even influenced the education which Shakespeare himself would have received at school.

The most memorable examples of public rhetoric in *Julius Caesar* are the two speeches in the Forum by Brutus and by Antony (Act III Scene ii). The language of the play as a whole is plain and straight-forward. Many of Shakespeare's greatest plays are much richer in metaphor and simile and more complicated in the organization of words within sentences. But Antony's speech to the crowd over Caesar's dead body is a masterpiece of oratory, simple in its language but devastating in its calculated effects.

These effects are partly a matter of language. They often involve the carefully-timed repetition of words and phrases, which begin to mesmerize the listeners, but which take on new meanings each time they are repeated (for example, 'honourable' is used with more and more sarcasm, so that it comes to imply its opposite, 'dishonourable').

But the effects are also a matter of long-term organization, so that effects many speeches ahead are borne in mind and 'nursed along' by Antony. Cassius shows how this kind of skill can work in a private conversation, when he slowly argues Brutus into considering the assassination of Caesar (throughout Act I Scene ii), and part of his skill is in his observation of how Brutus responds to everything that Cassius says to him. When Brutus hears a shout off-stage and blurts out 'I do fear the people/Choose Caesar for their king' (ll. 79–80) Cassius pounces on the word 'fear' and uses it to push Brutus a step down the road he would have him journey: 'Ay, do you fear it?/Then must I think you would not have it so '

Antony shows how to do the same thing in a public speech when he is in the Forum. He plays with the crowd, listening to them, challenging them, teasing them, seducing them. And, like Cassius, he does not rush his effects. He first refers to Caesar's will at III, ii, 129. It is 110 lines and 38 speeches (ten of them his own) later that he begins to tell them of its contents. By this point he can make his audience do anything he pleases.

The problem with rhetoric of the order of Antony's is that we come to distrust anything he has to say. When, at the end of the play, he delivers a funeral speech again, this time over the dead Brutus, we cannot know if he is paying Brutus a genuine tribute or mouthing platitudes because it is politic to do so. We are left unable to choose either alternative with any certainty, so chastened and wary are we after our experience of political life as *Julius Caesar* presents it.

FREEDOM

Once Caesar is dead, the conspirators cry out 'Liberty! Freedom! Tyranny is dead!' (III, i, 78). Some of them have purely personal grudges against Caesar, and if Cassius feels that Caesar restricts his freedom it is because Caesar oppresses his spirit and makes him envious. Cassius is living in the shadow of a man whose political success he resents. But Brutus joins the conspiracy out of an ideal, the ideal of political freedom.

In Brutus' opinion Caesar may be about to accept the crown. If he were to do this, the Senate and the people of Rome would have relinquished all political power to one man. This would be tyranny, and Brutus, along with every other Roman citizen, would have been deprived of his rights and freedoms. For Brutus, therefore, the death of Caesar means liberty. The Republic will have survived.

What happens, though, is that political freedom quickly degenerates into anarchy. Antony deliberately abandons his control of the mob in the Forum scene (III, ii) and does what he had vowed he would do, 'let slip the dogs of war' (III, i, 273). The ultimate victory of the Second Triumvirate at Philippi is a step towards the day when Octavius will become Emperor, and the Republic will be dead.

But political freedom is not the only freedom with which the characters of *Julius Caesar* are concerned. One of the most famous lines in the play, 'Beware the ides of March' (I, ii, 18; 23), suggests both that Caesar is bound to be in danger on that day and that he is free to avoid that danger. This raises the question of whether or not a man is free to control his own destiny.

Soothsayers, omens, portents, horoscopes, and even belief in the power of the gods to control men's lives, can all be regarded as evidence that men do not think that they are entirely free agents in this world. Caesar is sufficiently confident of his own powers as an earthly ruler to be tempted to believe that he has no need to fear the warnings of the Soothsayer. He refuses to be frightened by his priests into not attending the Senate. They claim that it is ominous that one of their sacrificial offerings should have been found to have no heart. Calphurnia pleads with Caesar: although she has never believed in omens ('I never stood on ceremonies': II, ii, 13) a frightening dream and the reports of bizarre events in the streets and in the skies now make her fear for her husband's safety. Caesar dismisses all this as so much superstition. Yet it was he who ordered the priests to read the entrails, and at II, i, 195 Cassius had remarked how Caesar 'is superstitious grown of late'.

Cassius has a most interesting shift in opinion about superstition and man's freedom of action. He is an Epicurean, a follower of the ideas of the Greek philosopher Epicurus (341–271 B.C.), who argued that men are free, that the gods have no interest in human affairs, and that men must therefore reject all superstitious belief in omens and portents.

Cassius tells Brutus that he thinks men are responsible for their own fates and cannot shift that responsibility to supernatural influences, such as the position of the planets at the time of a man's birth (I, ii, 138–40). Epicurus also wanted men to lose all fear of death and concentrate on achieving happiness in this life. So, during the storm scene (I, iii), Cassius walks the streets fearlessly, despite the lightning and the apparent signs of anger in heaven. His mind is set on ridding himself of what he considers to be a *real* threat, namely Caesar.

Nevertheless, at Philippi Cassius begins to feel apprehensive. Two eagles which had followed his army from Sardis, and which had seemed to be good omens, have now flown off and been replaced by birds of carrion. Cassius suddenly feels that this is a sign that he will lose the impending battle. Furthermore, he is impressed by the irony that it is his birthday. In other words, he has become superstitious and, further-more, fears death. He admits to Messala (V, i, 76–7) that he has changed his philosophical ideas: he is no longer an Epicurean.

Brutus' philosophy is closer to that of the Stoics. (The earliest of these Greek philosophers, Zeno, was a contemporary of Epicurus.) Where Epicurus had asserted man's freedom to control events, Stoicism stated that man has no control over what happens to him because all events are entirely predestined. Man's freedom lies merely in the fact that he has reason and can control his mental and emotional response to the events that are imposed upon him.

Although Stoicism seems to take away man's freedom and preaches a fatalistic attitude to life, in fact it is insistent that men *choose*. They must choose to submit to events without giving way to emotion. Pleasure and pain, good fortune and ill fortune, must be endured with the same fortitude and indifference. Just as Cassius finds that his experience in the play makes him question his Epicurean beliefs, so Brutus finds that his Stoicism is severely tested by events. When he hears of Portia's death, he is depressed by grief and loses his temper with Cassius. Cassius comments wryly, 'Of your philosophy you make no use,/If you give place to accidental evils' (IV, iii, 143–4).

Stoicism shares with Epicureanism a belief that death is not to be feared. But Stoics like Brutus' father-in-law, Cato, committed suicide rather than fall into the hands of their enemies and be forced to undergo the indignity of dying at the command of other men. Suicide represents a kind of ultimate freedom. However fatalistic Stoicism claimed to be, it recognized that, under certain circumstances, suicide could bring credit to a man. By ending his own life before his enemies have the chance to kill him, a man is refusing to surrender his freedom to control his destiny.

Brutus seems at one moment (V, i, 100–107) to be arguing that suicide is the coward's way out. Yet he chooses to die on his own sword, and Strato comments that this makes him free, 'For Brutus only overcame himself,/And no man else hath honour by his death' (V, v, 56–7).

HONOUR

'They that have done this deed are honourable.' Antony's repeated use of the term 'honourable' in his speech in Act III Scene ii forces his audience (both the audience in the Forum and the modern audience in the theatre) to consider what honour really is. At its most superficial the term describes social standing; Caesar's assassins are all respected Senators, the equivalent in Shakespeare's day of the sort of people who might be addressed as 'your honour'.

But Antony is suggesting that the conspirators are men to be honoured for their noble qualities. Or, rather, his tactic is to talk *as if* this were his opinion of them, then gradually to undermine the idea and turn the term 'honourable' into a sarcastic sneer. By the end of his address to the crowd gathered in the Forum 'honourable' has acquired the force of a term of abuse. We know that he is actually saying that Brutus and the other conspirators are *dis*honourable.

To be honoured is to be respected. Shakespeare seems to want us to decide how far we can respect each of his major characters. Is the Caesar he portrays really worthy of the solemn respect he is publicly accorded? Is the disrespect expressed by Flavius and Marullus, then Cassius, Casca and Decius, the result of honourable disagreement over political policies or of dishonourable envy and hate? Are Antony's dealings with the conspirators honourable? Is his encitement of the mob to frenzied anarchy honourable? Is his treatment of Lepidus honourable? Is he to be honoured for doing all these things in honour of Caesar's spirit?

The character who comes under the cruellest scrutiny in this respect is Brutus. He, after all, attempts to behave with honour throughout. He takes utterly seriously the notions of the honour of Rome, the honour of his family name, and his own personal honour, i.e. his own self-respect. By a terrible irony he argues himself into the position of killing Caesar. What could be more dishonourable than to butcher your own friend? Caesar cannot believe it – '*Et tu, Brute?*' Yet, for Brutus, it is the only honourable thing to do.

Shakespeare's Romans measure themselves against a strict standard of honour and manliness. Like Caesar, Brutus and Cassius and Antony have to prove themselves in two arenas, the theatre of politics and the theatre of war. Self-control and physical courage are, for them, essential elements in honourable manhood. Even Portia, being the daughter of a famous follower of Stoicism, tries to live up to this standard. And when they are facing military defeat, both Brutus and Cassius wish to protect their own honour, their good names and their self-respect, by not becoming prisoners of Antony and Octavius but taking their own lives and thereby demonstrating their independence and courage.

By the end, even Antony can see the nobility, honesty and gentility in Brutus. He pays him the honour of exclaiming 'This was a man!' (V, v, 75). Octavius gives Brutus a soldier's burial, 'ordered honourably' (V, v, 79). By honouring him in this way, there is momentary honour not only for Brutus but also for those who have triumphed over him.

Examination Questions

1. Read the following passage, and answer **all** the questions printed beneath it:

CASSIUS When Caesar lived, he durst not thus have moved
  me.
BRUTUS Peace, peace! You durst not so have tempted him.
CASSIUS I durst not?
BRUTUS No.
CASSIUS What, durst not tempt him?
BRUTUS   For your life you durst
                            not.   5
CASSIUS Do not presume too much upon my love;
  I may do that I shall be sorry for.
BRUTUS You have done that you should be sorry for.
  There is no terror, Cassius, in your threats;
  For I am armed so strong in honesty   10
  That they pass by me as the idle wind,
  Which I respect not. I did send to you
  For certain sums of gold, which you denied me;
  For I can raise no money by vile means;
  By heaven, I had rather coin my heart,   15
  And drop my blood for drachmas, than to wring
  From the hard hands of peasants their vile trash
  By any indirection. I did send
  To you for gold to pay my legions.
  Which you denied me; was that done like Cassius?   20
  Should I have answered Caius Cassius so?
  When Marcus Brutus grows so covetous,

To lock such rascal counters from his friends,
Be ready, gods, with all your thunderbolts,
Dash him to pieces!
CASSIUS   I denied you not.   25
BRUTUS You did.
CASSIUS   I did not. He was but a fool
That brought my answer back. Brutus hath rived my heart.
A friend should bear his friends' infirmities,
But Brutus makes mine greater than they are.

  (i) Give in your own words the meaning of lines 10–12 (*For I am armed . . . respect not*), and lines 22–3 (*When Marcus Brutus . . . from his friends*).
  (ii) What do we learn from Brutus, later in the scene, which could have contributed to his ill-temper at this point?
  (iii) Why do Brutus and Cassius quarrel? Who do you think is in the right, and why?

  2. Read the following passage, and answer **all** the questions printed beneath it:

ANTONY Good friends, sweet friends, let me not stir you up
To such a sudden flood of mutiny.
They that have done this deed are honourable.
What private griefs they have, alas, I know not,
That made them do it. They are wise and honourable,   5
And will, no doubt, with reasons answer you.
I come not, friends, to steal away your hearts:
I am no orator, as Brutus is,
But, as you know me all, a plain blunt man,
That love my friend; and that they know full well   10
That gave me public leave to speak of him.
For I have neither wit, nor words, nor worth,
Action, nor utterance, nor the power of speech,
To stir men's blood; I only speak right on.

I tell you that which you yourselves do know,   15
Show you sweet Caesar's wounds, poor poor dumb mouths,
And bid them speak for me. But were I Brutus,
And Brutus Antony, there were an Antony
Would ruffle up your spirits and put a tongue
In every wound of Caesar that should move   20
The stones of Rome to rise and mutiny
ALL We'll mutiny.
FIRST PLEBEIAN We'll burn the house of Brutus.
THIRD PLEBEIAN Away, then! Come, seek the conspirators.
ANTONY Yet hear me, countrymen; yet hear me speak.   25
ALL Peace, ho! Hear Antony, most noble Antony!
ANTONY Why, friends, you go to do you know not what.
    Wherein hath Caesar thus deserved your loves?
    Alas, you know not! I must tell you, then:
    You have forgot the will I told you of.   30

(i) Give in your own words the meaning of lines 17–21 (*But were I Brutus ... mutiny*).

(ii) *Most noble Antony* (line 26): what was the attitude of the crowd towards Antony just before he began his funeral oration on Caesar?

(iii) *A plain blunt man* (line 9): how far is this your impression of Antony here and in the play as a whole?

(*Oxford Local Examinations, 1980*)

3. Choose two of the following passages (*a*)–(*c*) and answer the questions which follow them.

(*a*) CAESAR   He reads much,
            He is a great observer, and he looks
            Quite through the deeds of men. He loves no plays,
            As thou dost, Antony; he hears no music;
            Seldom he smiles, and smiles in such a sort
            As if he mocked himself, and scorned his spirit
            That could be moved to smile at anything.
            Such men as he be never at heart's ease

Whiles they behold a greater than themselves,
And therefore are they very dangerous.
I rather tell thee what is to be feared
Than what I fear; for always I am Caesar.

(i) Of whom is this said? Do earlier events in the play suggest that Caesar has judged his character accurately?

(ii) Immediately before this speech, what type of man has Caesar said he prefers?

(iii) What personal physical weakness is revealed by Caesar in the rest of this speech? What contrast does this revelation create with the last two lines quoted above?

(*b*) BRUTUS O Antony, beg not your death of us.
Though now we must appear bloody and cruel,
As by our hands and this our present act
You see we do, yet see you but our hands
And this the bleeding business they have done.
. . .
CASSIUS Your voice shall be as strong as any man's
In the disposing of new dignities

(i) In what terms has Antony just addressed the conspirators? How do you explain his attitude to them at this point?

(ii) What do these remarks of Brutus and Cassius reveal about their characters?

(iii) What difference of opinion arises later in this scene between Brutus and Cassius?

(*c*) BRUTUS   Countrymen,
My heart doth joy that yet in all my life
I found no man but he was true to me.
I shall have glory by this losing day
More than Octavius and Mark Antony
By this vile conquest shall attain unto.

(i) What recent events have prompted Brutus to say 'I found no man but he was true to me'?

(ii) Would you include Cassius among those who were 'true' to Brutus? Give brief reasons for your answer.

(iii) Do the speeches of Antony and Octavius which end the play support Brutus' claim in the last three lines quoted here?

(*Southern Universities' Joint Board, 1974*)

4. How far does the play *Julius Caesar* illustrate the view that politics is a dirty game?

5. How far do you agree that although Portia and Calphurnia have little or no effect on what happens in the play *Julius Caesar*, they are very necessary characters in it?

(*Oxford and Cambridge Schools Examinations Board, 1982*)

6. 'So are they all, all honourable men.' How true do you think this statement is of any **two** of the conspirators?

7. Discuss Shakespeare's treatment of **either** flattery **or** super-stition in *Julius Caesar*.

(*Oxford and Cambridge Schools Examinations Board, 1982*)

8. 'Cassius is the mastermind of the conspiracy but its eventual failure is due to his faults of character.' What is your view about this statement?

9. Imagine you are a journalist for the *Rome Herald*. Report on interviews you have had with two or more Roman citizens after Caesar's funeral.

(*Oxford and Cambridge Schools Examinations Board, 1979*)

10. Several characters in the play refer to Brutus as the 'noble Brutus'. How far do you find him a noble figure?

11. How far do you accept Antony's description of himself as 'a plain blunt man'?

(*Oxford Local Examinations, 1978*)

12. 'Caesar dominates the play both before and after his death.' Write a study of the part played by Caesar and say how far you agree with this statement.

13. Describe how Cassius recruits Brutus to the conspiracy and show the skill with which Cassius uses his knowledge of Brutus and seizes his opportunitics.

(*University of London Schools Examination Board, 1980*)

14. What do the mob-scenes contribute to *Julius Caesar*?

(*Oxford Local Examinations, 1980*)

MORE ABOUT PENGUINS, PELICANS
AND PUFFINS

For further information about books available from Penguins please write to Dept EP, Penguin Books Ltd, Harmondsworth, Middlesex UB7 0DA.

In the U.S.A.: For a complete list of books available from Penguins in the United States write to Dept DG, Penguin Books, 299 Murray Hill Parkway, East Rutherford, New Jersey 07073.

In Canada: For a complete list of books available from Penguins in Canada write to Penguin Books Canada Ltd, 2801 John Street, Markham, Ontario L3R 1B4.

In Australia: For a complete list of books available from Penguins in Australia write to the Marketing Department, Penguin Books Australia Ltd, P.O. Box 257, Ringwood, Victoria 3134.

In New Zealand: For a complete list of books available from Penguins in New Zealand write to the Marketing Department, Penguin Books (N.Z.) Ltd, Private Bag, Takapuna, Auckland 9.

In India: For a complete list of books available from Penguins in India write to Penguin Overseas Ltd, 706 Eros Apartments, 56 Nehru Place, New Delhi 110019.